C000264779

Passenger Liners in Colour

DAVID L. WILLIAMS AND RICHARD DE KERBRECH

Ian Allan
PUBLISHING

HIGHLAND PRINCESS

(2/1930) Royal Mail Lines
14,216grt; 544ft 6in (165.9m) loa x 69ft 2in (21.1m) beam
102 First-class & 342 Third-class
Harland & Wolff, Belfast
2 x Oil 4DA 8-cyl Burmeister & Wain (by builder): 10,000bhp

The *Highland Princess*, fifth of the 'Highland' class, was launched at Belfast on 11 April 1929 and entered service 10 months later, in February 1930. She had nine years on the 'La Plata' service before World War 2, seven under the Royal Mail house-flag, and a further twelve postwar. War service, like that of the *Highland Monarch* (qv) and her other sisters, was as a troopship. Photographed here as she arrives off the Tilbury Landing Stage, she is seen turning in the river, using her port bow anchor as a pivot. In 1959, the *Highland Princess* was sold to John S Latsis, Piraeus and renamed *Marianna*. The intention had been to place her on a Genoa to Australia route, via Suez, but in the event this did not transpire. Instead, she was re-sold in 1960 to Czechofracht (Czechoslovak Ocean Shipping Co) of Prague and renamed *Slapy*. The fact that her new country of registry was land-locked may have influenced a further sale in the same year, to the state-owned fleet of the People's Republic of China. Registered in Shanghai, she was renamed *Guanghua*, occasionally written in the form *Guang Hua*. The former *Highland Princess* was still listed in Lloyds Register in 1980. Later, it was reported unofficially that she had been broken up between 1980 and 1981. *Kenneth Wightman*

First published 2007

ISBN (10) 0 7110 3204 1
ISBN (13) 978 0 7110 3204 0

All rights reserved. No part of this book may be reproduced or transmitted in any form or by any means, electronic or mechanical, including photocopying, recording or by any information storage and retrieval system, without permission from the Publisher in writing.

© Ian Allan Publishing Ltd 2007

Published by Ian Allan Publishing

an imprint of Ian Allan Publishing Ltd, Hersham, Surrey, KT12 4RG
Printed in England by Ian Allan Printing Ltd, Hersham, Surrey, KT12 4RG

Code: 0705/B1

Explanatory Notes

Preceding each caption or group of captions is a block of technical and date information relating to the named and featured ship or ships. The layout of this information where known, is as follows:

The vessel's name, (month and year built); former names with the (year) in which the name changes occurred; the vessel's owners;

the vessel's vital statistics: tonnage, length and beam in feet and inches with the equivalent (metric values);

the vessel's passengers, by class;

the vessel's builders and shipyard location;

the engine installation, the engine builders and, the horsepower output.

Abbreviations

Throughout, the following abbreviations have been adopted:

2SA	Two-stroke single acting
4DA	Four-stroke double acting
4SA	Four-stroke single acting
bhp	brake horsepower
cyl	cylinders
DR	Double Reduction gearing
ft	feet
grt	gross registered tonnage
HP	High Pressure
ihp	indicated horsepower
in	inches
IP	Intermediate Pressure
loa	length overall
LP	Low Pressure
m	metres
shp	shaft horsepower
SR	Single Reduction gearing
UDI	Unilateral Declaration of Independence

Introduction

This book is a celebration in colour of the many distinctive British ocean passenger liners that once – barely a generation ago – graced the sea-lanes of the world. Serving a vast route network, built up from the days of Empire, they were simply incomparable.

The number of British passenger liners on the register back in the late 1950s and early 1960s was quite staggering, well over 100, and the names of the companies that owned and operated them reads like a 'Who's Who' of the maritime elite. However, this was a period that witnessed the onset of decline of traditional route service passenger shipping and it is a matter of regret that these shipping lines were slow to react to the changing nature of overseas travel. Unlike foreign concerns, they failed to switch to dedicated cruise ships soon enough. By the time it was appreciated that the industry was heading in that direction it was already too late for many and one after the other these renowned companies disappeared forever.

This book is a tribute, too, to the quality of workmanship that produced these liners, at a time when British shipbuilding was truly second to none. British shipyards, now largely but a memory, then enjoyed full order books, a situation which may have caused complacency when it came to the need to invest in modern equipment and technology in the face of growing competition from the Far East. Nevertheless, such a failing cannot detract from the reality that many of the best passenger ships in the world came from British shipyards. Sad to say, that is no longer the case.

To demonstrate just how high the standard of construction of these vessels was, among those illustrated in the pages that follow are ships of a longevity that few passenger liners have attained. Only in recent years, when almost 50 years old, the last of Cunard's *Saxonia* class along with the seemingly ageless *Southern Cross*, all built in the 1950s, were finally sold for breaking up. What a testimony to John Brown's yard on Clydebank and to Harland & Wolff at Belfast, which were responsible for these ships. It is a similar story for the passenger liners built at Cammell Laird; Barclay, Curle & Co; Swan Hunters; Fairfields; Alexander Stephen and many other famous but now defunct yards. Many of these liners had second and third careers under foreign flags, long after the duties for which they were originally intended came to an end.

As with other types of ship, the immediate postwar period was one of considerable change for the ocean passenger liner, reflected particularly in hull design and engine type, as well as in ship-board amenities. At the beginning of the period covered here (the late 1950s onwards) there remained a number of vessels of prewar origin and even earlier, still sporting tall, thin, natural draught funnels, lofty masts and counter sterns. By the end of the period (the early 1970s) the majority of ships were of postwar construction or had been modernised, featuring squat funnels for forced draught boilers, and rounded and enclosed superstructures. The engines-aft arrangement, pioneered in the early part of the 20th century by Matson Lines, was reprised in the *Southern Cross* and her later consort, *Northern Star*, as well as in the ubiquitous *Canberra*.

Ironically, given that this was the period in which scheduled passenger liner services would fall into near-terminal decline, it was also the era in which onboard passenger amenities went through their most dramatic improvements. It is fitting here to summarise some of those enhancements introduced to make ocean travel a more comfortable and pleasurable experience.

Comfort being, perhaps, the highest priority, the installation of fin stabilisers to reduce motion and of air-conditioning to reduce the stifling heat of tropical voyages were particularly welcome. As a matter of interest, while some earlier ships had been fitted with punkah-louvre ventilation ports, many passengers resorted to the simple expedient of jamming a projecting and forward-facing piece of cardboard into their portholes so that air would be force-circulated around their cabins through the ship's forward movement.

On later liners built for the transatlantic run, promenade decks tended to be plated in, partly in preparation for air-conditioning but also to permit a modicum of shelter when taking the air during crossings in the depths of winter.

The technical specifications with each picture caption reveal how the numbers of classes of passengers carried were progressively reduced, this phasing out of social stratification manifested primarily in the virtually complete eradication of the lowest standards of accommodation. An aspect of this of direct benefit to those passengers who had occupied lower category cabins was the gradual eradication of communal ablutions in parallel with the introduction of en suite bathroom and toilet facilities.

An area of improvement long-neglected but today an essential dimension of any cruise holiday was passenger entertainment, particularly important on longer voyages. Today's cruise ships have ballrooms, cinemas and show theatres that rank with the best to be found in the West End or on Broadway but, as recently as the mid-1960s, it was still very much a matter of home-grown or holiday camp-style entertainment on the passenger liners. Bingo, fancy dress balls, horse racing and whist drives were very much the order of the day and lounges had to be temporarily adapted for matinee film showings prior to the introduction of the first purpose-built amenities on that final generation of luxury passenger liners.

British liners, given their numbers, were an eclectic mix of ships of all sizes. On most routes, though, the new liners were generally larger than their predecessors. For example, the *Canberra* and *Oriana* introduced on the Antipodes services, and the *Windsor Castle* for the Cape route, were almost double the size of earlier ships operated by their owners. Whereas in the prewar years the average size of ship for most passenger services had been of the order of 10-15,000 gross tons, in the postwar era it rose to 20-25,000 gross tons.

Of course, there is the matter, too, of what constitutes a passenger liner, especially when a vessel carries a substantial volume of cargo besides having accommodation for fare-paying passengers. Here, for instance, the Bibby ship *Leicestershire*, with spaces for just 75 passengers, has been included, whereas Shaw Savill's *Gothic*-class quartet, which for a time could carry 85 in First-class, have not. Generally speaking, any vessel with permanent cabin space for 12 or more passengers working a fixed route is classed as a passenger liner, but whether such borderline vessels should be described as being more cargo ship than passenger ship is open to interpretation. The rule of thumb could be whichever trade they predominantly serve but no doubt certain ships have been depicted in these pages that could fall on either side of that rather arbitrary definition.

Today, the world's cruise fleet is, with just one exception, powered by either diesel or diesel-electric engines or, as part of an emerging trend, by gas turbine-electric or combined gas turbine-electric and diesel powerplants. Very much dictated by present-day fuel costs, this is starkly different to the situation that existed fifty or sixty years ago when the majority of British ocean liners were powered by steam turbines. There were of course exceptions to this on certain routes, notably the Mail service to South Africa where motorships were commonplace. But even here, Union-Castle reverted to steam turbines for its last five express passenger vessels, while Royal Mail Lines took the almost unprecedented step of converting the innovative *Alcantara* and *Asturias*, motor vessels completed in the 1920s, from diesel to steam engines for technical reasons. The dominance of the geared steam turbine in the period covered by the book will be immediately apparent in the technical specifications that accompany each photograph.

It is often said that it is better to look forward than to look back, a positive observation that cannot really be argued with. It is also said that the British tend to be preoccupied with nostalgia and, as a consequence, have not embraced the new technological age with quite the enthusiasm of other nations. Certainly, a common perception is that something lost forever tends to be recalled with increasingly greater favour as the years pass. It was our primary aim in this book, as it was with the previous titles in this series, to bring into the public domain hidden treasures of maritime photography – pictures for the most part never seen before, displayed here in all their glory. The fact that they depict ships which exhibited a certain stylishness that stimulated the visual senses and which, in the past, inspired many great writers and poets to wax lyrical about their design attributes, is purely coincidental.

It is certainly not our intention here to deride, by comparison with its forebears, the modern passenger cruise ship whose emergence, it has to be said, has caught the imagination of a new generation of young ship enthusiasts and ocean travellers alike, for there have been many very elegant new cruise ships commissioned in recent times. Rather, our intention here is to present, without sentimentality, the equally grand liners from that earlier period when ocean passenger travel took a quite different form. Thus, it is with no apology that we offer the visual delights of a bygone era that follow. Calling to mind Kipling's 'great steamers of white and gold' and Priestley's 'giant liners of formidable power and real beauty', only those wonderful British passenger liners could have evoked such literary acclamation!

David Williams and Richard de Kerbrech
Isle of Wight,
March 2007

CALEDONIA
(3/1948) Anchor Line
11,255grt; 506ft (154.2m) loa x
    66ft 5in (20.2m) beam
326 First-class & 80 Steerage-class
Fairfield, Govan
2 x Oil 2SA 4-cyl Doxford
    (by builder): 14,000bhp

The *Caledonia* was a postwar sister of the prewar liners *Circassia* and *Cilicia*, the former being the first motorship to be built for Anchor Line. As with other vessels of the company she was designed for the UK to India and Pakistan service, operating from Liverpool to Port Said, Aden, Karachi and Bombay. An innovation for its day was the installation of partial air-conditioning in the main accommodation areas. She was sold by Anchor in 1965 to become a student hostel in Amsterdam and later scrapped at Hamburg during 1970. The photograph shows the *Caledonia* alongside at West Float, Birkenhead. Her paintwork appears pristine so she may have just completed a refit in either the Gladstone Dry Dock at Liverpool or at Cammell Laird's in Birkenhead. *Kenneth Wightman*

CILICIA
(5/1938) Anchor Line
11,172grt; 506ft (154.2m) loa x 66ft 6in (20.3m) beam
320 First-class & 80 Steerage-class
Fairfield, Govan
2x Oil 2SA 4-cyl Doxford (by builder): 14,000bhp

The *Cilicia* was launched on 21 October 1937, a sister to the *Circassia*. On 15 October 1939 she was commissioned as an Armed Merchant Cruiser (AMC) and was designated HMS *Cilicia*. She served in this role for 4½ years, then as a troopship for the remainder of the War. Following the War she continued in the UK to India and Pakistan service until 1965 when she was sold to the Netherlands and became a hostel for dockworkers in Rotterdam, renamed *Jan Backx*. This role lasted for 15 years until, during 1980, she was sold for scrapping in Spain. In this view the *Cilicia,* newly-painted and dressed overall, is high and dry in the Gladstone Dry Dock at Liverpool, probably just prior to flooding and return to service. *Kenneth Wightman*

DERBYSHIRE *(Above right)*
(10/1935) Bibby Line
10,641grt; 501ft 6in (152.9m) loa x 66ft 3in (20.2m) beam
115 First-class
Fairfield, Govan
2x Oil 2SA 8-cyl Sulzer (by builder): 8,000bhp

The last of a group of five four-masted motor liners built between 1926 and 1935 for the Bibby company's Burma trade, the *Derbyshire* originally sported a tall thin funnel more typical of steamers of the prewar era. She entered service in November 1935. Her class featured Bibby's 'Tandem System' cabins, an innovation introduced earlier by the company whereby even inside cabins had a porthole to the sea, accessed through a narrow passage to the ship's side. It was a real boon for passengers before the air-conditioning era. The *Derbyshire* was requisitioned as an AMC in November 1939. In 1942 she became a troopship and in 1943 was converted again, into a Landing Ship Infantry LSI(L). Following the War she was given a major overhaul in which she was fitted with a more squat motorship-type funnel, while two of her masts were removed. Besides her passenger accommodation, she had a cargo capacity of 535,880ft³. Returned to the Liverpool-Rangoon route, which she maintained for some fifteen more years, she arrived at Hong Kong on 18 February 1964 for demolition. This photograph shows the *Derbyshire* in her postwar configuration, off Tilbury. *Mick Lindsay*

LEICESTERSHIRE *(Below right)*
(12/1949) Bibby Line
8,922grt; 498ft (151.8m) loa x 60ft
    4in (18.4m) beam
75 First-class
Fairfield, Govan
2 x Steam turbines DR geared to a
    single screw (by builder):
    shp not known

The *Leicestershire*, along with her sister *Warwickshire,* the first pair of postwar vessels built for the Bibby Line, were also the company's first ships for many years to be turbine driven. The *Leicestershire* differed slightly from her sister in that she had an extra pair of derrick posts aft in place of a mainmast. The sister liners maintained the Liverpool to Rangoon route via Port Said, Port Sudan, Aden and Colombo. The *Leicestershire* was sold in 1965 to Typaldos Lines of Greece and renamed *Heraklion*. On 8 December 1966, whilst on passage from Crete to Piraeus, she was battered by heavy seas in the Aegean Sea that caused her to capsize and sink, one of the earliest examples of a ferry flooding through the failure of doors on the car deck. Of the 281 people on board her only 47 survived. The photograph of the *Leicestershire* in the Mersey Docks was taken prior to 1958 because the Pacific Steam Navigation Co's *Reina del Pacifico* may be seen in the background. In some reference sources, it is stated that Bibby's funnel colours were 'shrimp pink with black top'.
Kenneth Wightman

STAFFORDSHIRE

(1/1929) Bibby Line
10,018grt; 500ft 6in (152.6m) loa x 62ft 2in (19.0m) beam
Fairfield, Govan
109 First-class
2x Oil 2SA 8-cyl Sulzer (by builder): 7,700bhp

When completed the *Staffordshire* was originally fitted with four masts and a tall thin funnel, like the *Derbyshire*. Diesel propulsion proved a wise choice at the time as it suited the long voyages between the UK and Rangoon. The *Staffordshire* was operated on the Burma run until 1940. In March 1941 she was damaged by German bombers off the Scottish coast and beached but, following salvage and repairs on the Tyne, she was employed as a troopship from January 1942 to November 1948. She was then rebuilt by Fairfield with her mainmast removed and her mizzen and after masts replaced by derricks. A new broader, squat funnel was also fitted. In 1959 she was sold for demolition in Osaka and renamed *Stafford Maru* for the voyage to Japan. The photograph shows her amidst a fleet of lighters in the Tilbury Dock. Although she was virtually identical to her sister *Worcestershire,* her lifeboats were stowed one deck lower than on that vessel. *Kenneth Wightman*

DEVONSHIRE *(Right)*

(7/1939) Bibby Line (managed for Ministry of Transport)
12,773grt; 516ft 10in (157.5m) loa x 63ft 3in (19.3m) beam
130 First-class, 96 Second-class & 99 Third-class, plus berths for 824 troops
Fairfield, Govan
2x Oil 2SA 8-cyl Sulzer (by builder): 6,500bhp

The *Devonshire* was a purpose-built prewar troopship completed, along with the British India-managed *Dilwara* and *Dunera*, and P&O-managed *Ettrick*, to a similar, virtually standard design. She originally carried 104 First-class and 90 Second-class passengers along with 1,500 troops. As such she left the UK in 1939 and did not return until 1944, engaged throughout that period trooping to Mediterranean, African, Far Eastern and Australian ports. She also took part in the Sicily landings. During 1953-1954 she was refitted at Fairfields, having her accommodation layout completely updated. From that time, her troop accommodation took the form of three-tier standee bunks in dormitories. In January 1962, British India Line acquired her for conversion by Barclay Curle, Glasgow into the school cruise ship *Devonia* (page 14) (qv). Here the *Devonshire* is seen in her troopship livery at Southampton, flying her Bibby Line houseflag from the jackstaff. In the background may be seen either of Elders & Fyffes' *Camito* or *Golfito. Kenneth Wightman*

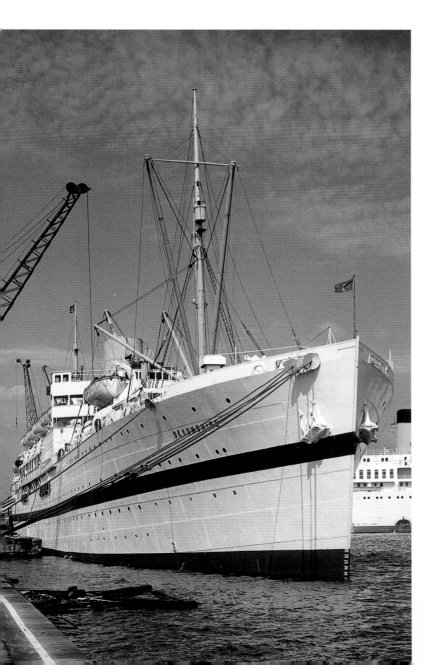

OXFORDSHIRE

(2/1957) Bibby Line (managed for Ministry of Transport)
20,586grt; 609ft 5in (185.7m) loa x 78ft 3in (23.8m) beam
220 First-class, 100 Second-class & 180 Third class, plus berths for 1,000 troops
Fairfield, Govan
4 Steam Turbines DR geared to twin screws (by builder): 18,000shp

The *Oxfordshire* was the last purpose-built British troopship constructed for service between the UK and her overseas possessions, entering service in February 1957. The Ministry of Transport bore a share of her operational costs. Her completion marked the end of a long association between Bibby and the company's preferred builders, the Fairfield Shipbuilding and Engineering Co. After the termination of her contract with the MoT, at the end of 1962, the *Oxfordshire* was chartered by Bibby Line to a subsidiary of the Sitmar Line, Italy, for the emigrant service to Australia, beginning in February 1963. During May of that year she was taken in hand in the Netherlands for conversion into a full passenger ship at a cost of £4.5million, with accommodation for 1,870 passengers in a single class, following which she was purchased by the Fairstar Shipping Corp and renamed *Fairstar*. In the event, Harland & Wolff at Southampton were engaged to complete the rebuilding work. On 19 May 1964, she entered the UK-Australia service. Later, on 20 August 1973, she made her first cruise from Sydney, subsequently being dedicated to this type of work with her passenger numbers reduced to 1,300. The Sitmar Group was bought by P&O on 1 September 1988 and, befitting her new owners' business organisation, the *Fairstar* operated exclusively for the Australian market. Sold on 11 February 1997 for breaking up, she was renamed *Ripa* for the delivery voyage to India, arriving at Alang on 10 April 1997 for the commencement of demolition. Here the *Oxfordshire* is seen at Southampton while still serving as an MoT troopship.
Kenneth Wightman

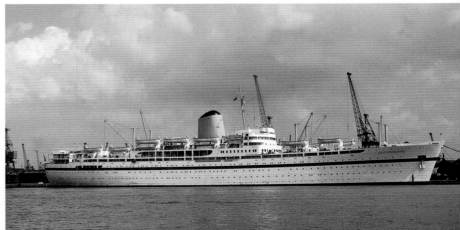

CENTAUR

(1963) Blue Funnel Line
8,262grt; 480ft 9in (146.5m) loa x
   66ft 3in (20.2m) beam
200 First-class
John Brown & Co, Clydebank
2 x Oil 2SA 11-cyl by Burmeister
   & Wain, Copenhagen:
   16,500bhp

This significant ship from the 1960s was designed to carry passengers in addition to animals and refrigerated cargo. She was initially operated between Fremantle and Singapore, carrying 4,500 Australian sheep and 40 dairy cows outbound, returning to Fremantle via North Western Australia with up to 700 cattle. A limited amount of high-standard passenger accommodation was also provided in either direction. It was the first time since the War that a Blue Funnel ship had been fitted with B&W diesels, and the *Centaur* was also extraordinary in that, because of her fine lines and bulbous bow, she could maintain a service speed of 20 knots. From 1973 she was owned by the China Mutual SN Co, a subsidiary of Alfred Holt, operating until 1978 under Eastern Fleets of Singapore. Between 1978 and 1985 she transferred to Blue Funnel (Sea) Pty of Singapore and while with these owners, in 1982, she was chartered by Kernow Shipping on the South African run when their vessel *St. Helena* was taken up for the Falklands War. She duly had her funnel painted with Kernow Shipping's heraldic sea lion logo. In 1985, the *Centaur* was sold to Shanghai Haixing Shipping Co of China, with whom she operated for 14 years. At first named *Hai Long*, these same owners renamed her *Hai Da* during 1986. In 1999 she was sold within China to the China Development Co Ltd, the intention being further trading but this did not come to pass. Records dating from February 2006 reveal that unspecified Chinese interests sold her for breaking up, although demolition may already have been completed sometime earlier. This undated photograph shows the innovative *Centaur* resplendent in her tropical Blue Funnel livery while serving as a unique passenger cargo livestock carrier. *Mick Lindsay*

ANSELM
(9/1950) ex *Thysville* (1961) ex
Baudouinville (1957) Booth
Line
10,854grt; 505ft (153.9m) loa x
64ft 10in (19.8m) beam
248 one-class
Cockerill, Hoboken
Oil 2DA 8-cyl Burmeister & Wain
(by builder): 9,250bhp

This vessel started life as the *Baudouinville* with the Compagnie Maritime Belge on their route to the Belgian Congo, Central Africa, making her maiden voyage from Antwerp to Matadi on 19 September 1950. Following the Congo's independence she was renamed *Thysville* on 1 June 1957. That year, her engine was refitted with turbochargers that increased power output by more than 2,000bhp and raised her speed to 16½ knots. Redundant on her formal colonial trade, in February 1961 she was sold to the Booth Line of Liverpool for £800,000 and renamed *Anselm*. She entered the Liverpool and Portugal to Barbados, Trinidad, and North Brazil (including the River Amazon) route. By 1963 she was transferred within the Vestey Group, of which Booth Line was a part, to the Blue Star Line. Renamed *Iberia Star*, she was refitted by Bremer Vulkan for the London to River Plate service. During 1965 she was again renamed, becoming the *Australasia*, and then placed on the Singapore to Melbourne route for the Austasia Line, yet another part of the Vestey Group. In 1972 she was sold for breaking up in Taiwan and sailed there at the end of that year to commence demolition at Hualien on 18 March 1973. This photo of the *Anselm* was taken in May 1963 alongside the Hamburg berth of Bremer Vulkan, prior to her transfer to Blue Star. *Kenneth Wightman*

DILWARA

(1/1936) British India Line
  (managed for Ministry of
  Transport)
12,555grt; 517ft (157.6m) loa x
  65ft (19.8m) beam
325 in three classes, plus berths for
  705 troops
Barclay Curle & Co, Glasgow
2x Oil 2SA 5-cyl Doxford (by
  builder): 6,500bhp

Owned and operated by British India, the *Dilwara* was the prototype of a series of four purpose-built troopships ordered by the Ministry of Transport by the then Minister, Hore-Belisha. Diesel-powered, they were apparently intended for exclusive cruise employment when not trooping. A sister-ship, the *Dunera* soon followed. Initially her accommodation layout provided for 104 First and 100 Second Class passengers together with 1,150 troops, but throughout World War 2 the troop complement was increased to 2,300. In 1952 she was given a major refit and modifications in which new three-tier standee bunks were installed to accommodate a smaller number of troops, increasing her gross tonnage. With the cessation of carrying soldiers by designated troopship in 1960, she was sold to the China Navigation Co of London and in October that year sailed to Hong Kong where she was refitted in the Taikoo Shipyard for pilgrim voyages to Jeddah. She was refurbished to carry 243 First and 1,669 pilgrims or, when used for cruising, 200 passengers alone. From 1961 she was deployed on the Malaysia to Jeddah run with occasional cruises between Hong Kong and Auckland. On 1 December 1971 she arrived at Kaohsiung, Taiwan to be scrapped. This view of the *Dilwara* at Southampton shows that her original well deck forward had been built up as part of the 1952 refit. *CCQ*

DUNERA

(8/1937) British India Line
12,615grt; 516ft 10in (157.5m) loa
   x 63ft 2in (19.2m) beam
190 cabin passengers plus 800
   dormitory berths
Barclay Curle & Co, Glasgow
2x Oil 2SA 5-cyl Doxford (by
   builder): 6,500bhp

When built the *Dunera* was the second of a trio of troopers built by Barclay Curle – the third being P&O's *Ettrick* – and her passenger and troop capacity were the same as that of the *Dilwara*. Early in World War 2, the *Dunera* conveyed so-called enemy aliens from Liverpool to Australia, among them a large group of Jews who came to be known as the 'Dunera Boys'. Her wartime troop capacity, like that of her sister, was increased to 2,300, and she too came through the six-year conflict unscathed. Following the War she was given a major refit to meet new peacetime standards. During this she was fitted with three-tier standee bunks for 835 troops with additional accommodation for 320 paying passengers in three classes, raising her gross tonnage. In 1961, at the end of her troopship era, she was refitted as a school cruise ship by Palmers Hebburn Co, which included the installation of specially fitted-out classrooms. It was the MP Tam Dalyell who, then a teacher, suggested this use for the redundant troopship. In April 1961 she made her inaugural 14-day cruise as a school ship. After six successful seasons, in November 1967 she arrived at Bilbao in Spain to be broken up. This view of the *Dunera* as a school ship, flanked by two London Tugs, was taken in October 1967, making it one of the last photographs taken of her before she went to the breakers. *Kenneth Wightman*

DEVONIA
(7/1939) ex-*Devonshire* (1962) British India Line
190 cabin passengers plus 830 pupils in dormitory
  berths
Other details as for the *Devonshire*

Here the former Bibby Line troopship *Devonshire* is shown in British India livery as the school ship *Devonia*. The conversion of other former troopships like the *Dunera* and the *Nevasa* to school ships became a significant development in the British educational system at that time, offering as it did a range of thematic educational cruises in European waters. For the *Devonia* this activity lasted for only five years but the experience set the trend for other liners that followed. Soon after its conclusion she arrived at La Spezia on 14 December 1967 for demolition. *Mick Lindsay*

KAMPALA

(8/1947) British India Line

10,304grt; 507ft (154.5m) loa x 66ft 3in
 (20.2m) beam

60 First-class, 180 Second-class & 80 Third-
 class plus 800 unberthed passengers

Alexander Stephen & Son, Glasgow

6 Steam Turbines SR geared to twin screws
 (by builder): 9,700shp

The *Kampala* was one of a pair of sisters built for British India Line to replace an earlier pair of the same name built in 1931 for operation on the Bombay to East Africa service, which extended as far as Durban. She was launched in December 1946, followed in March 1948 by her sister *Karanja*. When they entered service, their hulls were painted black but during the 1950s they were repainted white in keeping with a fleet-wide change embracing all British India passenger-carrying vessels. The pair were then employed mainly on routes from UK to Indian Ocean ports and from India to East Africa. In the run-up to the assimilation of much of the British India fleet within the P&O Group, the *Kampala*, surplus to the company's requirements, was made redundant. Sold for scrapping, she arrived at Kaohsiung, Taiwan on 24 July 1971. This view shows the *Kampala* sailing out of the Thames bound for South Africa, flying the Royal Mail pennant. *CCQ*

KENYA

(8/1951) British India Line
14,464grt; 539ft 10in (164.5m) loa
  x 71ft 5in (21.8m) beam
194 First-class & 103 Tourist-class
Barclay Curle & Co, Glasgow
6 Steam Turbines SR geared to
  twin screws (by builder):
  12,300shp

When launched on 28 November 1950, the *Kenya*, along with her sister *Uganda*, were the largest liners built for British India. They originally sported a black hull. The *Kenya* made her maiden voyage from London on 22 August 1951 on British India's East African service, calling at Gibraltar, Malta, Port Said, Aden, Mombassa, Zanzibar, Dar-es-Salaam and Beira. This proved to be a successful route enjoying constant colonial traffic and it survived the threat raised by the Mau Mau emergency. In 1955 her hull was painted white along with other passenger ships of the company. Political developments in Africa in the mid-1960s undermined her trade and this became a lean period for the *Kenya*. 'Uhuru' and independence in Kenya in 1964, followed by UDI two years later in Rhodesia, leading to the Beira patrol off Mozambique, resulted in the curtailment of her itinerary. Prematurely surplus to requirements she was withdrawn from service and on 2 July 1969 she arrived at La Spezia to be broken up. Resplendent in her white livery in this view of her in London's Royal Albert Dock, she is handling cargo, probably prior to sailing. *Kenneth Wightman*

UGANDA

(7/1952) British India Line
14,430grt; 539ft 10in (164.5m) loa
x 71ft 5in (21.8m) beam
167 First-class & 133 Tourist-class
Barclay Curle & Co, Glasgow
6 Steam Turbines SR geared to
twin screws by Wallsend
Slipway: 12,300shp

The *Uganda* was launched on 15 January 1952 and completed in July the same year. She was the 450th ship to be built for British India since the company's formation in 1856. She attained a creditable 19¼ knots on trials and had partial air-conditioning installed. Completed a year later than sister-ship *Kenya,* she had a slightly different internal layout and her funnel was 12ft taller. On 2 August 1952 she sailed on her maiden voyage on the London to Beira service. As for the *Kenya,* employment on the East African colonial run at first proved to be successful but later, as aspirations for independence among African countries resulted in political tensions, the service proved difficult to maintain and cost her patronage. On 5 April 1967 the *Uganda* arrived at Howaldtswerke at Hamburg where she was extensively refitted as a school ship for 1,224 pupils, at a cost of £2.8 million. This view shows the *Uganda* pre-1967, in her original state with two masts, alongside at the Royal Albert Dock, London. *Kenneth Wightman*

UGANDA
16,907grt
1,224 schoolchildren
Other details as
   previous page

The *Uganda* departed on her first school-ship cruise on 27 February 1968. The formation of the P&O Passenger Shipping Division in 1972 led to her registration along with all other surviving British India ships under the P&O Group banner, the British India company identity being relegated to a trade-name for educational cruises. On 10 April 1982 she was requisitioned for service during the Falklands campaign and hastily converted into a hospital ship at Gibraltar before sailing to the South Atlantic. As such, her funnel was painted buff with a Red Cross on it and crosses were also painted on each side of her hull. During her two-month auxiliary deployment the *Uganda* treated 730 casualties, 103 of whom were Argentinians, besides the first casualties from HMS *Sheffield* who were conveyed to her by helicopter. The *Uganda* arrived back at Southampton as a troopship on 13 July 1982 and, following a refit at North Shields she was chartered in this role for a further two years before being laid up on the River Fal on 4 May 1985. On 29 April 1986 she was sold to Triton Shipping Co. St Vincent, renamed *Triton* and destined for Kaohsiung, where she arrived on 15 July 1986, for demolition. Five weeks later, she was driven aground by typhoon 'Wayne' but, though practically careened, scrapping subsequently ensued. This photograph shows the *Uganda* newly converted as a school ship with extended accommodation forward and classrooms on her boat deck so she could fulfill the combined role of educating children while cruising. Air-conditioning was extended to all her accommodation areas as part of the 1967 conversion. *Mick Lindsay*

NEVASA

(7/1956) British India Line
20,527grt; 609ft 3in (185.7m) loa
   x 78ft 3in (23.8m) beam
307 cabin passengers plus 783
   pupils in dormitory berths
Barclay Curle & Co, Glasgow
6 Steam Turbines, HP & IP DR
   geared and LP SR geared to
   twin screws (by builder):
   20,280shp

British India's fifth major postwar liner, the *Nevasa*, was designed primarily for trooping with an accommodation layout for 220 First-class, 100 Second-class, and 180 Third-class passengers, plus 1,000 troops. She was delivered in July 1956, the company's centenary year, and became the first troopship to be fitted with stabilisers and to have her hospital spaces air-conditioned. The Ministry of Transport bore the majority of her running costs under the charter to ferry troops to British colonial possessions but she became a costly option as transportation by air increased and she was laid up in the River Fal from 13 October 1962. The following year the MoT prematurely terminated their 15-year charter with the company, and formally returned the *Nevasa* to British India. The company had her rebuilt as a school ship between 1964 and 1965 by Silley, Cox & Co of Falmouth, and she departed Southampton on 28 October 1965 on her first voyage in this capacity. After British India was fully assimilated into the P&O Group in 1972, her new owners continued to run the *Nevasa*'s educational cruises for another three years. Having completed barely 20 years total service, she arrived at Kaohsiung on 30 March 1975 to be broken up. The *Nevasa* is shown in her British India livery while serving as a school ship. The disposal of the *Nevasa* and the *Uganda*, the last of the school ships, brought this unique and valuable programme to an end. *Mick Lindsay*

EMPRESS OF FRANCE
(5/1928) ex-*Empress of India*
   (1947) ex-*Duchess of Bedford*
   (1947) Canadian Pacific Line
20,448grt; 601ft 3in (183.3m) loa
   x 75ft 3in (22.9m) beam
218 First-class & 482 Tourist-class
John Brown, Clydebank
6 Steam Turbines SR geared to
   twin screws (by builder):
   21,000shp

The *Empress of France* initially entered service as the *Duchess of Bedford,* one of four sisters for Canadian Pacific's Atlantic service, the others being the *Duchess of Atholl*, *Duchess of Richmond* and *Duchess of York*. She made her maiden voyage from Liverpool to Montreal on 1 June 1928. On 30 August 1939 she was taken up as a troopship and made her first auxiliary voyage from Liverpool to Bombay. She and her sister *Duchess of Richmond* survived the War, the only two of the quartet to do so, and on completion of her wartime role she arrived at Fairfield, Glasgow in March 1947 for a major refit. She was renamed *Empress of France* and re-entered the service from Liverpool to Montreal on 1 September 1948. In the summer season, she operated to Montreal but in the winter she terminated at St. John, New Brunswick. Between 1958 and 1959 she underwent a complete refit in which her funnels were slightly tapered and topped by cowls, and her masts and lifeboats were repainted white. This new guise was short-lived, however, as she was sold in 1960 for demolition in Newport, Monmouthshire. The *Empress of France* is seen here in the Gladstone Dock at Liverpool on 31 August 1956, handling cargo from her forward hold. *Kenneth Wightman*

EMPRESS OF SCOTLAND
(6/1930) ex-*Empress of Japan*
  (1942) Canadian Pacific Line
26,313grt; 666ft 6in (203.1m) loa
  x 83ft 10in (25.6m) beam
458 First-class & 250 Tourist-class
Fairfield Shipbuilding &
  Engineering Co Ltd, Govan
6 Steam Turbines SR geared to
  twin screws (by builder):
  34,000shp

Originally built as the *Empress of Japan* for Canadian Pacific's trans-Pacific route, she commenced her maiden voyage from Liverpool to Quebec on 14 June 1930. She entered service on the Pacific in August 1930 and in so doing became the fastest liner on the route. She was taken up for troopship duties on 26 November 1939 and was renamed *Empress of Scotland* on 16 October 1942 as a consequence of Britain being in a state of war with Japan. At the end of her troopship service, she arrived at Liverpool on 3 May 1948 and was then refitted at Liverpool and Glasgow for return to peacetime service on 9 May 1950, working from Liverpool to Quebec. During November the following year she conveyed Princess Elizabeth and the Duke of Edinburgh back to the UK after their Canadian tour. During April 1952 her masts were shortened to allow passage up the St Lawrence as far as Montreal. Six years later, in January 1958, she was retired by Canadian Pacific and sold to the Hamburg-Atlantic Line for which she was reconstructed and modernised at Howaldtswerke, Hamburg as the *Hanseatic*. Her three funnels were replaced by two, her length was increased to 673 ft (205.2m), and her gross tonnage raised to 30,030. She maintained the Cuxhaven, Southampton and New York service until 7 September 1966 when an engine room fire while at New York spread through her, causing extensive damage. Towed back to Hamburg, where she was assessed as beyond repair, on 2 December 1966 the *Hanseatic* was sold for demolition locally. This view shows the *Empress of Scotland* in her heyday alongside the Gladstone Dock at Liverpool, about to sail for Canada. She was then one of only three surviving British liners to have three funnels. *CCQ*

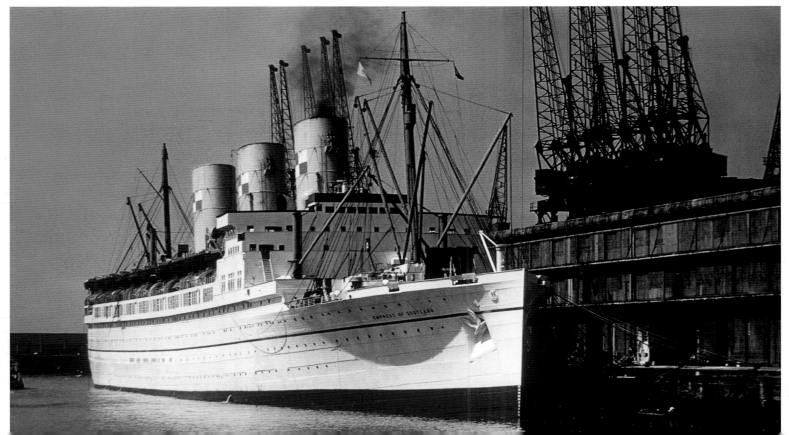

EMPRESS OF BRITAIN

(3/1956) Canadian Pacific Steamships Ltd
25,516grt; 640ft (195.1m) loa x 85ft (25.9m) beam
160 First-class & 894 Tourist-class
Fairfield, Govan
6 Steam Turbines DR geared to twin screws (by builder): 30,000shp

Her Majesty the Queen launched the *Empress of Britain*, Canadian Pacific's first new liner postwar, on 22 June 1955. She was fitted with stabilisers from new and was the first ship built in Great Britain to be completely air-conditioned. The first of a postwar trio of *Empress* liners ordered by Canadian Pacific, with her sisters she brought an upgrade in comfort and style for passengers on the Liverpool to Canada route. Following two short 'shakedown cruises', she sailed on her maiden voyage from Liverpool to Montreal on 20 April 1956. Less than a decade later, through increased competition from air travel and the decline in passengers on the Atlantic run, she was sold to the Greek Line in 1964, to replace their *Arkadia*, the former *Monarch of Bermuda*, and was renamed *Queen Anna Maria*. She was given a six-month refit at the Mariotti shipyards in Genoa over the winter of 1964-1965 during which her accommodation was altered to carry 1,313 in two classes or 741 during cruises. She made her first voyage from Piraeus to New York on 24 March 1965. The *Queen Anna Maria* was laid up at Piraeus in January 1975 and sold in December that year to the fledgling Carnival Cruise Lines of Panama, which renamed her *Carnivale*. After making her first Carnival cruise in February 1976, she remained with the company until 1993. Since then she has been repeatedly sold and renamed: *Fiesta Marina* for TSS Fiestamarina, Bahamas (1993-1994), *Olympic* for Turquoise Sea Shipping Inc, Greece (1994-1998) and *The Topaz* for Topaz International Shipping Inc, Panama (1998-2006). Early in 2006 she was chartered to the Japanese Peace Boat organisation without further change of name. On 20 April 2006 she had been in service for 50 years. This photograph, taken some time before 1965, shows the *Empress of Britain* in the Gladstone Dock, Liverpool, flying her Royal Mail pennant, outward bound for Canada. *Kenneth Wightman*

FRANCONIA
(6/1923) Cunard Line
20,341grt; 624ft (190.2m) loa x
    73ft 8in (22.4m) beam
253 First-class & 600 Tourist-class
John Brown & Co, Clydebank
6 Steam Turbines DR geared to
    twin screws (by builder):
    13,500shp

The *Franconia* was launched on 21 October 1922 for Cunard's North Atlantic service from Liverpool, one of a pair with later sister *Carinthia*. As with other liners of the company she was frequently used for cruising during the 1930s and her hull was painted white while so engaged. She was taken up for troopship duties in September 1939 and was deployed for the duration in most areas of the world. In February 1945 she was used as the Headquarters ship for Prime Minister Winston Churchill during his attendance at the Yalta Conference. The *Franconia* was returned to Cunard in August 1948 and sent for an extensive refit after her lengthy wartime service. She re-entered the Liverpool to Quebec route on 22 June 1949, following modifications that significantly reduced her passenger numbers, which, from that time, were accommodated in two rather than three classes. After seven years' more service, she was withdrawn and sold for demolition at Inverkeithing where she arrived on 18 December 1956. The *Franconia* is immaculately painted in this view, possibly taken at Southampton, which was her home port during her latter years. *CCQ*

BRITANNIC

(6/1930) Cunard Line
27,778grt; 711ft 9in (216.9m) loa
x 82ft 5in (25.1m) beam
427 First-class & 564 Tourist-class
Harland & Wolff, Belfast
2 x Oil 4DA 10-cyl Burmeister &
Wain (by builder): 20,000bhp

The *Britannic* along with her sister, the *Georgic*, were the last liners to be built for Cunard's former rival, the White Star Line. As built she was the second largest motorship in the world after the Italian liner *Augustus* and she carried 1,550 passengers in three classes. Despite the merger between White Star and Cunard in 1934, she retained her original livery through to the end of her career and she continued to operate mainly on the Liverpool-New York service. On 19 April 1935 she made her first voyage from London to New York. Even before World War 2 had broken out, on 30 August 1939, she was taken up for troopship duties and during her time in this role she transported 173,550 passengers (mainly troops) and sailed some 324,972 miles! Following the war she was released back to her owners in March 1947 and given a major refit by Harland & Wolff at Liverpool. As returned to service, revamped as a two-class liner, her increased gross tonnage, at 27,666, made her the world's largest motorship of the day! Cracking of her bedplate girders and fatigue cracks in her main crankshaft hastened her demise. During 1960 she was sold for demolition, arriving at Inverkeithing on 19 December that year. The photograph shows the *Britannic* alongside the Huskisson Dock, Liverpool, preparing for another Atlantic crossing and blowing her Tri-tone whistle. As she nears the end of her operational career, her rust-streaked hull is in need of a 'paint job'. *Kenneth Wightman*

QUEEN MARY

(5/1936) Cunard Line
81,237grt; 1,019ft 6in (310.7m)
loa x 118ft 7in (36.1m) beam
711 First-class, 707 Cabin-class &
577 Tourist-class
John Brown & Co, Clydebank
16 Steam turbines SR geared to
quadruple screws (by builder):
200,000shp

The *Queen Mary*'s keel was laid down on 27 December 1930 as yard number 534. A year later, construction was suspended due to the Cunard company's financial difficulties and the world depression. Following the merger with White Star in 1934, work on her resumed that April and she sailed on her maiden voyage on 27 May 1936, the largest liner in the world. Three months later she gained the Atlantic Blue Riband from French Line's *Normandie* but conceded it to her rival in 1937. In August 1938, she completed the outward and homeward journeys at average speeds of 30.99 and 31.69 knots respectively, a record that stood until 1952. On the outbreak of World War 2, she was laid up in New York and later sailed to Sydney where she was converted into a troopship with a capacity for up to 10,500 men; a figure which, in practice, was exceeded by a considerable margin. Trooping duties commenced in May 1940 and took her to every part of the world. On 2 October 1942, she cut the light cruiser *Curacoa* in two during close manoeuvres, whilst being escorted off the North of Ireland, costing the lives of 338 of the cruiser's crew. The *Queen Mary* was released from Government service and returned to Cunard in September 1946. Her builders gave her an extensive overhaul and she returned to service on 31 July 1947. After a further 20 years service in consort with the *Queen Elizabeth*, she was sold to the city of Long Beach, California to become a hotel, museum and convention centre, departing Southampton for the last time on 31 October 1967. To this day, she remains in this final resting place. This photograph shows the *Queen Mary*, dressed overall and immaculately painted, making her final sailing from Southampton, on 31 October 1967, with the tug/tender *Gatcombe* in attendance. *Mick Lindsay*

QUEEN ELIZABETH
(3/1940) Cunard Line
83,673grt; 1,031ft (313.9m) loa x
    118ft 7in (36.1m) beam
823 First-class, 662 Cabin-class &
    798 Tourist-class
John Brown & Co, Clydebank
16 Steam Turbines SR geared to
    quadruple screws (by builder):
    200,000shp

Launched on the 28 September 1938 the *Queen Elizabeth* was almost complete in March 1940 when she sailed for New York to avoid being bombed, later continuing to Singapore to be fitted out as a troopship. At the time she was the largest liner ever to be built and the largest troopship available to the Allies, conveying troops to war theatres around the globe. Like the *Queen Mary* she sailed alone and unescorted because of her superior speed and during her wartime role she steamed some 1½ million miles. On 6 March 1946, she became the first Cunard ship to be released from war service and was immediately refitted as a luxury passenger ship, as originally intended, at Southampton and Gourock. The *Queen Elizabeth* eventually sailed on her maiden voyage from Southampton to New York on 16 October 1946, finally launching Cunard's two-ship express service, planned before the war. She was later fitted with Denny-Brown stabilisers and air-conditioning but by 1968 she was surplus to requirements and too big for cruising. That year she was sold to the Elizabeth Corporation of Port Everglades, Florida, to become a convention centre and tourist attraction, arriving there on 8 December 1968. On 19 July 1969 she was sold on to Queen Ltd for the same purpose and renamed *Elizabeth* but these owners went bankrupt a year later. She was then bought by Chinese shipowner C Y Tung, renamed *Seawise University* and left Florida on 10 February 1971 bound for Hong Kong to undergo a massive overhaul and conversion into a floating university. On 9 January 1972, when nearing the end of the refit, she caught fire and, completely gutted, capsized in Hong Kong harbour. Between 1974 and 1979 the wreck was salvaged and removed. The *Queen Elizabeth* is seen here in more halcyon days, departing Southampton for New York, being nudged by two Red Funnel tugs with another unseen tug on the bow line. *Mick Lindsay*

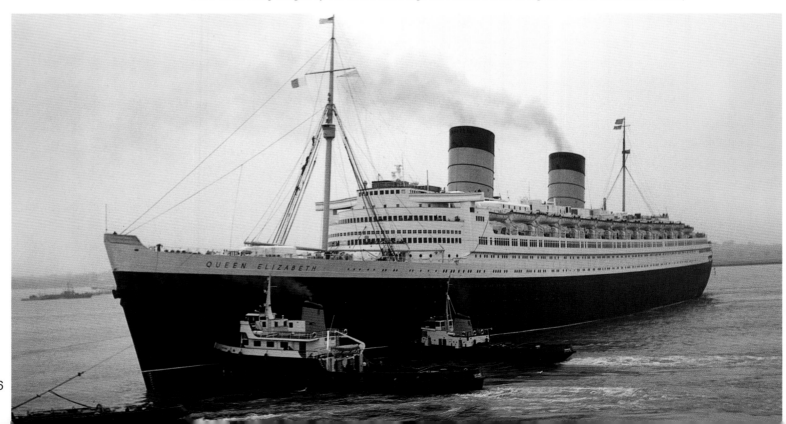

MEDIA
(8/1947) Cunard Line
13,345grt; 531ft 5in (162.0m) loa
   x 70ft 4in (21.4m) beam
250 First-class
John Brown & Co, Clydebank
4 Steam Turbines DR geared to
   twin screws (by builder):
   15,000shp

The *Media*, together with her Harland & Wolff-built sister *Parthia*, was built exclusively to cater for First-class clientele along with a substantial volume of cargo on a fortnightly service from Liverpool to New York. When she sailed on her maiden voyage to New York on 20 August 1947 she was Cunard's first postwar vessel. She was also the first trans-Atlantic liner to be fitted with stabilisers and all her public rooms were air-conditioned. The *Media* was sold in 1961 to Cogedar Line of Genoa and renamed *Flavia*. Following an extensive overhaul, lasting nearly a year, in which she was modernised to carry 1,224 passengers, she entered the Genoa-Sydney route. In 1969 she was sold to Costa Armatori for Miami-based cruising and then in 1982 to Panamanian interests when she was renamed *Flavian*, later changed to *Lavia*. After this she was laid up in Hong Kong where she was gutted by fire on 7 January 1989. Capsized onto her port side and beyond repair she was sold to Taiwanese shipbreakers. This atmospheric photograph of the *Media* was taken in the Mersey at Liverpool. *CCQ*

CARONIA

(12/1948) Cunard Line
34,172grt; 715ft (217.9m) loa x
91ft 5in (27.9m) beam
581 First-class & 351 Cabin-
class; 932 one-class while
cruising
John Brown & Co, Clydebank
6 Steam Turbines, HP DR geared
and IP & LP SR geared to
twin screws (by builder):
35,000shp

The *Caronia* was launched by Princess Elizabeth (now Her Majesty the Queen) on 30 October 1947. In a break from Cunard tradition she was painted in three shades of green and earned the nickname 'the Green Goddess'. Although she was intended primarily for luxury cruising from New York, she was also used on the North Atlantic service, making her maiden voyage from Southampton on 4 January 1949. The *Caronia* was partially air-conditioned later extended to the entire ship. She gained a reputation for her elaborate long-distance dollar-earning cruises and became the hallmark for luxury for the Company. During 1965 she was refitted and modernised at Belfast during which her accommodation was updated and an open-air swimming pool installed. In July 1968 she was sold to Universal Line SA of Panama and renamed *Columbia* and sent to Piraeus for a refit. Upon its completion she emerged as the *Caribia*. She commenced a programme of cruises to the West Indies but in March 1969 suffered an engine room explosion. Following prolonged lay up at New York, she was sold to Taiwanese shipbreakers, leaving New York on 27 April 1974 under tow for Kaohsiung. On 12 August 1974 she was driven onto the breakwater at Apra Harbour, Guam and broke up. This photograph shows the *Caronia* at Southampton in June 1963, with some of her lifeboats swung out for testing. In the adjacent Trafalgar drydock is Royal Mail's flagship *Andes*. *Kenneth Wightman*

CARONIA
Details as previous page

This second view of the *Caronia*, taken after her 1965 refit, shows her outward bound for New York. Ironically she was disposed of after less than 20 years' service at a time when cruising was starting to become fashionable. *Mick Lindsay*

SAXONIA

(8/1954) Cunard Line
21,637grt; 608ft 4in (185.4m) loa
  x 80ft 4in (24.5m) beam
110 First-class & 819 Tourist-
  class
John Brown & Co, Clydebank.
4 Steam Turbines DR geared to
  twin screws (by builder):
  24,500shp

The *Saxonia* was the first in a class of four ships built primarily for the Canadian service, which, at the time, were the largest Cunarders built for that route. They replaced six 'A' class ships that had been built in the 1920s. She made her maiden voyage from Liverpool to Montreal on 2 September 1954. The *Saxonia* initially operated out of London on the Canadian run but was switched to Southampton in June 1957. Between 1962 and 1963 she was refitted by John Brown and re-entered service as the *Carmania*, painted in three shades of green. Although still employed on the Canadian run, she cruised from the United States during the winter months. In 1967 she was painted all white and used exclusively as a cruise ship until put up for sale in December 1971. She was acquired in 1973 by the Soviet Union's Black Sea Shipping Co which renamed her *Leonid Sobinov*. From that time she was used for cruising out of Australia and New Zealand until sold for scrap during 1999. This quite rare photograph of the *Saxonia* shows her early on in her career, pre-1957, while operating out of London's Royal Albert Dock. Moored astern of her is Shaw Savill's *Taranaki. Kenneth Wightman*

CARINTHIA
(6/1956) Cunard Line
21,947grt; 608ft 3in (185.4m) loa
   x 80ft 4in (24.5m) beam
154 First-class & 714 Tourist-class
John Brown & Co, Clydebank.
4 Steam Turbines DR geared to
   twin screws (by builder):
   24,500shp

The *Carinthia* was the third of the John Brown-built quartet to enter service. She was launched on 14 December 1955 and sailed on her maiden voyage from Liverpool to Montreal on 27 June 1956. The route was switched from Liverpool to New York during the winter season. Along with her sisters she was repainted white during 1967 and switched to cruising. This was a short-lived diversion as she was sold in January 1968 to Fairland Shipping Corp of Liberia and renamed *Fairland* but, although intended for Sitmar's New Zealand route, she was laid up at Southampton's 101 berth for the next two years.

On 21 February 1970 she arrived at Trieste for a major transformation into a one-class cruise ship, re-entering service in July 1972 as the *Fairsea* for the Fairsea Shipping Corp, Monrovia. Bought by P&O on 1 September 1988 she was placed with the Princess Cruises Inc subsidiary as the *Fair Princess*. After leaving Princess Cruises in June 2000 she was involved in a number of changes of ownership until finally sold to Emerald Cruises Inc of Liberia and renamed *China Sea Discovery*. When just under fifty years old, she was sold to Indian breakers in August 2005 for $4.2 million. Renamed *Sea Discovery* for the delivery voyage, she arrived at Alang on 22 November 2005 for scrapping to commence. This view shows the *Carinthia* unloading in her homeport of Liverpool, her paintwork immaculate. *Kenneth Wightman*

SYLVANIA

(6/1957) Cunard Line
21,989grt; 608ft 3in (185.4m) loa
  x 80ft 4in (24.5m) beam
154 First-class & 724 Tourist-class
John Brown & Co, Clydebank
4 Steam Turbines DR geared to
  twin screws (by builder):
  24,500shp

The *Sylvania* was launched on 22 November 1956. Her delivery, in June 1957, completed what had been a lucrative order for a class of four sisters all built by John Brown. She sailed on her maiden voyage from Greenock to Montreal but thereafter her home port was Liverpool. Although designed for the Canadian service, she switched to the Liverpool to New York service during the winter months. As with the other liners of her class, she was painted white and utilised on cruising from 1967. In 1968, she was sold to the Fairwind Shipping Corp of Liberia to be placed on the New Zealand service but she was laid up, at Southampton's 101 berth, under the name *Fairwind*, alongside the *Fairland* ex *Carinthia*. On 14 January 1970 she arrived at Trieste for a major cruise ship conversion, re-entering service in this role along with her sister *Fairsea* and the *Fairstar* (ex *Oxfordshire*). In 1988 she was renamed *Sitmar Fairwind* and later that year, on 9 September, she was bought by P&O who renamed her *Dawn Princess* for operation by Princess Cruises Inc. Between 1993 and 2004 she was chartered to Phoenix Seereisen, a German cruise company, sailing under the name *Albatros*. Following this she was renamed *Genoa* and arrived at Alang, India on 6 January 2004 for demolition. This photograph shows the *Sylvania* on an overcast day during June 1967 resplendent in her cruising white. She is departing Southampton for Montreal with Red Funnel's *Thorness* nudging her bow. *Mick Lindsay*

CARMANIA
ex *Saxonia* (1963)
22,592grt
117 First-class & 764 Tourist-class
Other details as for the *Saxonia*.

Following her conversion from the *Saxonia*, the *Carmania* was initially painted in three shades of green, the livery introduced by Cunard's cruising standard-bearer, the *Caronia*. Her passenger accommodation was remodelled to suit more extensive cruise employment. During 1967 she was painted all white, as seen in this view of her at Southampton's 101 berth. Painters can be seen down aft touching up the paintwork. Later, the white hull was augmented with the corporate brand name 'CUNARD' located below the bridge, between decks 1 and 2. The *Carmania* was laid up for nearly two years from 1969, moored alongside the *Franconia* and Shaw Savill's *Southern Cross* near the King Harry Ferry on the River Fal. Subsequently, after 17 years' service with the Black Sea Shipping Co as the *Leonid Sobinov*, she passed to Transblasco Four Shipping of Malta. On 1 October 1999 she arrived at Alang in India for demolition. *Richard de Kerbrech*

FRANCONIA
ex *Ivernia* (1963)
22,637grt
119 First-class & 728 Tourist-class
John Brown & Co, Clydebank
4 Steam Turbines DR geared to twin
  screws (by builder): 24,500shp

In this picture, the *Franconia* is seen sporting her *Caronia* green cruising livery adopted in October 1962. In this guise, she made her first voyage from Rotterdam to Montreal on 1 January 1963. The photograph shows her lying idle at Southampton in July 1966 towards the end of the five-week-long British seaman's strike that had started in June. She is moored abreast of Shaw Savill's *Southern Cross* out of picture to the left. Prior to her sale to the Soviet Union in August 1973, she was laid up alongside the *Southern Cross* and the *Carmania* in the River Fal. In 1992, after nearly 20 years as the *Fedor Shalyapin*, she transferred to Odessa Cruise Co of Malta and was renamed *Salona*. Twelve years later, she was sold for scrap, demolition commencing on 6 February 2004. *Mick Lindsay*

QUEEN ELIZABETH 2

(4/1969) Cunard Line

65,863grt; 963ft (293.5m) loa x 105ft 3in (32.1m) beam

604 First-class & 1,223 Tourist-class or 1,740 one-class when cruising

John Brown & Co, Clydebank (latterly part of Upper Clyde Shipbuilders)

4 Steam Turbines DR geared to twin screws (by builder): 110,000shp

The following views, here and on the rear endpapers, show the *Queen Elizabeth 2*, Cunard's flagship, in three stages of her career as a steamship between 1969 and 1986.

The *Queen Elizabeth 2*, or QE2 as she has become more internationally known, was launched by Her Majesty the Queen on 20 September 1967. As a result of 'teething troubles' with her steam turbines her delivery to Cunard was delayed by four months. Built at a cost of £25,427,000, she was designed for a dual-purpose role, initially for 564 First-class & 1,441 Tourist-class on the Atlantic run or 1,400 passengers in a single class when cruising. These numbers were modified from 1972. The *Queen Elizabeth 2* sailed on her maiden voyage on 2 May 1969 from Southampton to New York. On 9 January 1971, while cruising in the Caribbean, she took part in the rescue of passengers and crew from the fire-engulfed French liner *Antilles*. This photograph shows the *Queen Elizabeth 2* in her original guise, departing Southampton for New York during October 1970. In May 1972 she was the victim of a hoax bomb scare that inspired the fictional film 'Juggernaut'. *Mick Lindsay*

QUEEN ELIZABETH 2
67,140grt
Other details as previous page

On 23 July 1976 an engine room fire off the Scilly Isles caused serious damage to her starboard engine and she put back to Southampton for repairs. Following the Argentine invasion of the Falkland Islands, the *Queen Elizabeth 2* was requisitioned by the British Government on 4 May 1982 for service as a troopship. She was hastily converted at Southampton with many of her fittings being removed and helicopter pads fitted fore and aft before sailing on 12 May. She embarked 5 Infantry Brigade, landing them at South Georgia on 27 May. After returning home she was given a refit before resuming her normal commercial service. This view shows her upon completion of that refit, in August 1982, with her hull painted shell grey and her funnel sporting the traditional Cunard livery. She is seen leaving Southampton with some of her lifeboats swung out, the tugs *Clausentum* and *Ventnor* in attendance. To the left, the passengers aboard Red Funnel's ferry *Netley Castle* get a grandstand view while en route to Cowes. *Mick Lindsay*

ACCRA
(9/1947) Elder Dempster Lines
11,599grt; 471ft (143.6m) loa x 66ft 2in (20.2m) beam
259 First-class & 24 Third-class
Vickers-Armstrongs, Barrow-in-Furness
2 x Oil 2SA 4-cyl Doxford (by builder): 9,400bhp

Ordered in February 1945 for Elder Dempster's Liverpool to Lagos service, the *Accra* and her sister *Apapa* replaced two 1926-built ships of the same names lost in World War 2. The *Accra* commenced her maiden voyage in September 1947. The photograph is believed to show her on the River Mersey with a Liverpool-Birkenhead ferry passing behind her stern. After making 171 round voyages to West Africa, the *Accra* was sold for breaking up at Cartagena, Spain from November 1967. *Kenneth Wightman*

APAPA

(3/1948) Elder Dempster Lines
11,607grt; 471ft (143.6m) loa x 66ft 2in
  (20.2m) beam
259 First-class & 24 Third-class
Vickers-Armstrongs, Barrow-in-Furness
2 x Oil 2SA 4-cyl Doxford (by builder):
  9,400bhp

The introduction of the *Apapa*, seen here, and *Accra* in 1947-1948 permitted the resumption of Elder Dempster's three-weekly sailing schedule to West Africa. Both had air conditioning installed in their passenger areas in 1960, a welcome improvement to passenger comfort. At the same time Third-class was adapted into Tourist-class. The *Apapa* survived in Elder Dempster service for one more season than her sister but was sold in September 1968 to Shun Cheong Steam Navigation Co of Hong Kong. Renamed *Taiphooshan*, she maintained a service between Hong Kong, Singapore and Penang for the next six years. She was scrapped at Kaohsiung, Taiwan in February 1975. *CCQ*

AUREOL

(10/1951) Elder Dempster Lines
14,083grt; 537ft (163.6m) loa x
    70ft 2in (21.4m) beam
353 Tourist-class
Alexander Stephen & Sons,
    Glasgow
2 x Oil 2SA 4-cyl Doxford (by
    builder): 10,800bhp

The addition of the *Aureol* to the Elder Dempster passenger fleet from 3 November 1951 allowed the company to increase its sailings from Liverpool to Nigeria to every other week. The *Aureol* was the largest passenger vessel to be owned by Elder Dempster Lines and she made the first ever cruise by any of the company's ships, in 1967. Completed with accommodation for 253 First-class and 100 Cabin-class passengers, from 1968 the *Aureol* was converted into a one-class Tourist ship. Just four years later, on 16 March 1972, she made her final voyage from Liverpool to Lagos, transferring to Southampton from where she made her inaugural sailing on 26 April 1972. A new schedule, involving ten round trips annually, was planned but because this was under-subscribed she was laid up from October 1974. A month later she was sold to Marianna Shipping & Trading, Panama. The photograph shows the *Aureol* making her final sailing from Southampton to West Africa in September 1974. Renamed *Marianna VI*, she was placed at Jeddah, Saudi Arabia, functioning as a workers' accommodation ship. Later, from February 1980, after a lengthy period of lay-up in Perama Bay, Piraeus, she became a pilgrim hotel ship based at Rabegh, a port further north on the Red Sea coast. This activity came to an end in December 1989, and the *Marianna VI* was once again laid up, in the Gulf of Eleusis, Greece. She was scrapped at Alang, India from 5 June 2001. *Mick Lindsay*

RUAHINE

(5/1951) Federal Steam Navigation
   Co (operated by New Zealand
   Shipping Co)
17,851grt; 584ft 6in (178.1m) loa
   x 75ft 2in (22.9m) beam
267 one-class
John Brown & Co, Clydebank
2 x Oil 2SA 6-cyl Doxford (by
   builder): 14,200bhp

The *Ruahine*, introduced to the New Zealand run from London on 22 May 1951, was a smaller version of the *Rangitoto* and *Rangitane* completed for the New Zealand Shipping Co two years earlier. She could be distinguished from her earlier fleetmates by the three lifeboats she had on each side, where the other pair carried four on each side. After fifteen years under the New Zealand Shipping Co house flag, on 1 January 1966 the *Ruahine* adopted the colours of Federal Line – her owners – transferring back to full operation by Federal a year later. In 1968, she was sold to the Orient Overseas Line (Chinese Maritime Trust, Taipeh), taking the new name *Oriental Rio*. Following reconditioning and modification at Hong Kong, she then spent the next four years, from February 1969, on a round-the-world service out of Hong Kong. The former *Ruahine* was broken up at Kaohsiung from December 1973. The *Ruahine* is seen here in the River Thames in October 1966 in Federal Line colours. *Kenneth Wightman*

QUEEN OF BERMUDA

(2/1933) Furness, Withy & Co
22,501grt; 579ft 6in (176.6m) loa x
   76ft 8in (23.4m) beam
700 First-class & 31 Second-class
Vickers-Armstrongs, Barrow-in-
Furness
Turbo-electric, comprising 2 x steam
   turbines by Fraser & Chalmers,
   Erith, connected to electric motors
   by General Electric Co, Witton,
   driving quadruple screws:
   20,000shp

In June 1931, the luxury liner *Bermuda*, in only her fourth season, was destroyed by fire at Hamilton, Bermuda. She had been so successful in her short career that her owners had already ordered a larger consort, the *Monarch of Bermuda*. Arising from the fire loss, a replacement ship was required and the *Queen of Bermuda*, a sister of the *Monarch*, was commissioned, joining her from February 1933. These were truly luxurious liners, as reflected in their extraordinary passenger ratio, and nothing was spared in the splendour of their interior fittings. Their service, linking New York with Hamilton, was rightly dubbed 'The Millionaires Run'. Six years on the route by the *Queen of Bermuda* were followed by war service in which she and her sister served as Armed Merchant Cruisers and troopships. Cruise voyaging to Bermuda was resumed in February 1949 but by the *Queen of Bermuda* alone for her sister was gutted by fire while being reconditioned. Taken in hand for modernisation by Harland & Wolff, Belfast, in 1961, the *Queen of Bermuda* emerged from the shipyard with an extended bow and a single raked funnel. The *Queen of Bermuda* was finally broken up at Faslane in December 1966, ending a successful 33-year long career and terminating the millionaires cruise service. The *Queen of Bermuda* and *Monarch of Bermuda* featured turbo-electric propulsion, a system not widely adopted but one which freed up space within the hull by eliminating the requirement for an astern turbine. *Mick Lindsay*

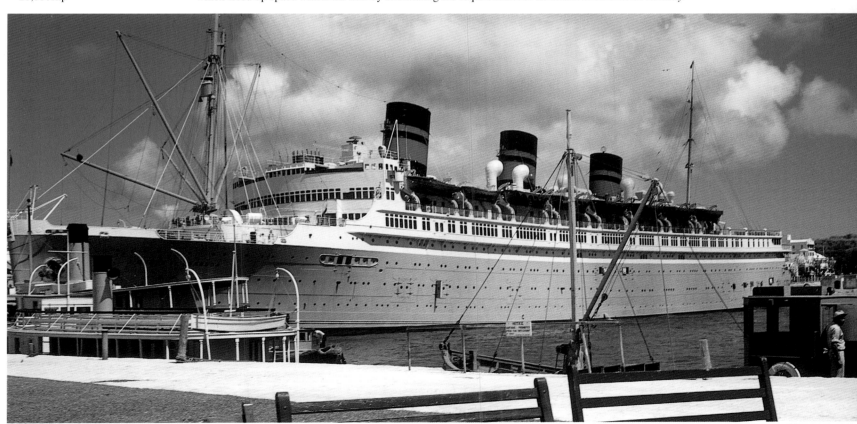

EMPIRE KEN

(1928) ex *Ubena* (1945) Ministry of
Transport (managed by Royal Mail
Lines)

9,523grt; 487ft (148.4m) loa x 60ft 3in
(18.4m) beam

Blohm & Voss, Hamburg

4 x steam turbines SR geared to a single
screw (by builder): shp not known

The Ministry of Transport owned a large fleet of troop carriers in the 1950s, maintaining overseas garrisons in the last days of Britain's status as a colonial power. The numbers were swollen by several former German ships ceded to Great Britain in 1945 as war reparations. Seen here in the Old Docks at Southampton, on 24 March 1956, is one such Government-owned vessel, the *Empire Ken*, which started life as the *Ubena* of the Deutsche Ost-Afrika Linie. Her first eleven years, on the round-Africa route, were followed by German wartime service as a U-boat mother ship, culminating in participation in the Operation 'Hannibal' evacuation of territories in the eastern Baltic. Completing seven round voyages, the *Ubena* rescued 27,170 persons from captivity by the Russians. The *Empire Ken* survived postwar for just twelve years, being sent to ship-breakers at Dalmuir, Scotland in September 1957. Also to be viewed in this scene are two Red Funnel tugs, the *Neptune* on the right and, in the distance to the left, the tender *Calshot*.
Kenneth Wightman

EMPIRE ORWELL

(12/1936) ex *Empire Doon* (1949) ex
    Pretoria (1945)
Ministry of Transport (managed by
    Orient Line)
18,036grt; 576ft 9in (175.8m) loa x 72ft
    4in (22.0m) beam
Blohm & Voss, Hamburg
6 x steam turbines SR geared to twin
    screws (by builder): 14,200shp

Another former German passenger ship serving postwar as a MoT troopship is the *Empire Orwell* ex *Pretoria*. She is secured alongside Berth 49, close to the entrance of the Trafalgar Dry Dock in Southampton Docks. As the *Pretoria*, from 19 December 1936, she had maintained the service from Hamburg to Capetown for the Deutsche Ost-Afrika Linie, along with her sister *Windhuk*. Her subsequent auxiliary service during the war, like the *Ubena*, concluded with evacuation work in the Baltic in the winter of 1944-45. Allocated to Great Britain, she was immediately deployed as the troop carrier *Empire Doon*, repatriating Allied servicemen, but engine breakdowns resulted in prolonged lay-up. In 1949, following a comprehensive refit and overhaul of her engines, she resumed troop transportation duties as the *Empire Orwell*, continuing until 1958 when she was chartered to the Pan Islamic Steamship Co, Karachi, to serve as a pilgrim carrier. It was an activity that was to dominate much of the remaining 25 years of her life. That November she was sold to Alfred Holt & Co (Blue Funnel Line) and renamed *Gunung Djati*. In 1962 she was sold to the Government of Indonesia, with further sales to P.T. Maskapai Pelajaran in 1965 and to P.T. Perusahaan Pelajaran in 1966, both companies with offices in Djakarta. The latter company had her converted into a motorship (12,000bhp MAN diesels) by Hong Kong United Dockyards in 1973. The former *Pretoria* was sold to the Indonesian Government for a second time in 1979, spending the next five years as the Navy accommodation ship *Kri Tanjung Pandan*, based at Tanjung Priok. Laid up at Singapore in 1984, she was scrapped in Taiwan three years later. *Kenneth Wightman*

REMUERA

(4/1948) ex *Parthia* (1962) New
   Zealand Shipping Co
13,619grt; 534ft (163.8m) loa x 70ft
   4in (21.4m) beam
350 First-class
Harland & Wolff, Belfast
4 x steam turbines DR geared to twin
   screws (by builder): 15,000shp

The one-time Cunard Line passenger-cargo ship *Parthia*, the first Cunarder to be built by Harland & Wolff, was acquired by the New Zealand Shipping Co in November 1961 and renamed *Remuera*. The extent of her modification for her new owners can be gauged by comparing this photograph with that of her former sister *Media* on page 27. As Cunard ships there had been a heavy dependence on their cargo capacity, at the expense of their passenger role. Thus, the New Zealand Shipping Co had the *Remuera* rebuilt aft by the Alexander Stephen shipyard in Glasgow, giving her additional passenger berths while simultaneously reducing her cargo spaces. The result was that her passenger numbers, all accommodated in a single class, increased by 100. After four years on the London to Wellington run, from 1 June 1962, the *Remuera* was sold to Eastern & Australian Steamship Co and renamed *Aramac*. She was placed on a service from Melbourne to Hong Kong, Yokohama and the Philippines, commencing in February 1965 but just four years later, in November 1969, she arrived at Kaohsiung to be broken up, yet another indication of the decline in route passenger shipping. *Kenneth Wightman*

REINA DEL PACIFICO

(3/1931) Pacific Steam Navigation Co
17,872grt; 574ft (174.9m) loa x 76ft
1in (23.2m) beam
280 First-class, 162 Second-class &
446 Third-class
Harland & Wolff, Belfast
4 x Oil 4SA 12-cyl Burmeister & Wain
(by builder): 22,000bhp

The largest Pacific Steam Navigation ship to date and the first to have a white hull, the *Reina del Pacifico*, was launched on 23 September 1930. She had a classic motor-ship appearance with two squat, horizontally level funnels, although the fore funnel was only a dummy to balance her profile. The *Reina del Pacifico* left Liverpool on her maiden voyage to Valparaiso on 9 April 1931, with calls at La Rochelle, Vigo, Hamilton, Havana, Kingston, Panama Canal, Guayaquil, Callao and Antofagasta. The homeward run followed the same route, although every year, commencing January 1932, it was broken by a round-South America voyage. On the outbreak of war, she was requisitioned as a troopship, serving in this capacity for the next six years, concluding her Government service with employment on repatriation duties. The *Reina del Pacifico* was released back to her owners in January 1947 for overhaul and refit at Belfast although her return to service was delayed until the end of 1948 because of an engine-room explosion during sea trials. Her last departure from Liverpool was on 27 April 1958, after which she was withdrawn and broken up at Newport, Monmouthshire. This view shows her at the Princes Landing Stage, Liverpool. *CCQ*

REINA DEL MAR

(4/1956) Pacific Steam Navigation Co
20,234grt; 600ft 9in (183.1m) loa x
    78ft 4in (23.9m) beam
207 First-class, 216 Cabin-class & 343
    Tourist-class
Harland & Wolff, Belfast
6 x steam turbines DR geared to twin
    screws (by builder): 17,000shp

Introduced on 3 May 1956 as the intended replacement for the *Reina del Pacifico*, for two seasons the *Reina del Mar* worked alongside her veteran fleet-mate on the run from Liverpool to South America, via Panama. Their itinerary was Liverpool to Valparaiso via France, the Caribbean, West Indies, Venezuela, Panama, Ecuador, and Peru; a gruelling schedule that enabled them to complete only four round trips a year. The *Reina del Mar* herself survived on the route for only seven years. She was fully air-conditioned and had been fitted with stabilisers from the outset. Chartered to the Travel Savings Association for a sequence of cruises in 1963, in March of the following year she was returned to her builders for conversion into a dedicated cruise ship. Placed under Union-Castle Line management, she was given accommodation for 1,047 passengers in a single class. She made her first cruise, post-conversion, on 10 June 1964. For her career from that point, see page 76. The photograph shows her pre-reconstruction, at Liverpool in 1963.
Mick Lindsay

OTRANTO

(12/1925) Orient Line
20,051grt; 658ft 7in (200.7m) loa x
    79ft (24.1m) beam
1,412 Tourist-class
Vickers, Barrow-in-Furness
6 x Steam Turbines SR geared to
    twin screws (by builder):
    20,000shp

The Orient Line had suffered the loss
of four of its ships during World War
1 and, partly to make good these
deficiencies, it embarked upon a
major new building programme in
the 1920s. Central to this was a five-
ship class of large two-funnelled
express ships, beginning with the
Orama of 1924 and followed by the
Oronsay, *Otranto*, *Orford* and
Orontes. Third of the class, the
Otranto entered the London to
Brisbane service on 9 January 1926.
Trooping service during World War 2
continued until 1948 when the
Otranto was overhauled and
reconditioned for civilian service by
Cammell Laird, Birkenhead. She
made her first postwar sailing, to
Sydney, on 14 July 1949. The
photograph shows her berthed in the
Tilbury Dock on 21 July 1956, still
looking in spotless condition.
Beyond her is one of the biscuit-
coloured postwar 'O' ships, thought
to be the *Orsova*. The *Otranto* was
sold for breaking up at Faslane in
June 1957. *Kenneth Wightman*

ORONTES

(7/1929) Orient Line

20,186grt; 663ft 8in (202.3m) loa
x 79ft (24.1m) beam

1,410 Tourist-class

Vickers-Armstrongs, Barrow-in-
Furness

6 x Steam Turbines SR geared to
twin screws (by builder):
20,000shp

Last of the *Orama*-class ships, the *Orontes* differed slightly from her earlier consorts and could be regarded as more of a half-sister. Where they had straight stems, she had a slight rake to her bow. Internally, a reduction in her passenger numbers had the effect of increasing space allocation per passenger, especially in First-class. Her maiden voyage on 26 October 1929 was followed by ten unbroken years on the London to Brisbane service and then seven more as a World War 2 troopship. Overloaded shipyards immediately after the war forced shipping lines to seek capacity wherever it could be found to get their vessels overhauled for peacetime service. For the *Orontes*, Orient Line unusually contracted Thornycroft at Southampton to undertake her refit and, work complete, she returned to the London to Sydney route on 17 June 1948. Subsequently converted into a one-class Tourist ship in 1953, the *Orontes* survived until March 1962 when she was sold to be broken up in Valencia, Spain. The *Orontes* is also seen in the Tilbury Dock but in her case she looks in a poorer state of maintenance compared with the *Otranto* in the previous picture. *Kenneth Wightman*

CORFU

(9/1931) P&O Line
14,280grt; 543ft (165.5m) loa x 71ft 5in (21.8m) beam
181 First-class & 213 Tourist-class
Alexander Stephen & Sons, Glasgow
6 x Steam Turbines SR geared to twin screws (by
    builder): 14,000shp

P&O commissioned the sister liners *Corfu* and *Carthage* in 1931 for the London to Hong Kong service. They were similar in many respects to the earlier *Cathay*, *Comorin* and *Chitral* built for the Australia route but, unlike the earlier trio, steam turbine plant replaced quadruple expansion steam reciprocating machinery. The *Corfu* and *Carthage* were taken over as Armed Merchant Cruisers in November 1939, primarily used for convoy escort duties, serving with the Royal Navy until 1944 when they were converted into troopships for the Ministry of War Transport. The *Corfu* returned to the Hong Kong service from 1949 to 1961 but, as reconstructed postwar, she was reduced to a single funnel (she had entered service with two) and her accommodation spaces were extended in the forward part of her hull in the space previously occupied by a well-deck. She also shed her original black livery, adopting a white hull and yellow funnel, colours universally applied to P&O's postwar passenger fleet. The photograph shows the *Corfu* in her postwar configuration. Taken in the King George V Dock, London, in the 1950s, a Brocklebank cargo vessel can also be seen further along the quayside. In August 1961, the *Corfu* was sold for demolition in Osaka, Japan, making the voyage to the scrapyard under the name *Corfu Maru*. Her sister had preceded her to the same breakers three months earlier. *Kenneth Wightman*

STRATHMORE
(9/1935) P&O Line
23,580grt; 665ft 1in (202.7m) loa
    x 82ft 3in (25.1m) beam
497 First-class & 487 Tourist-class
Vickers-Armstrongs, Barrow-in-
    Furness
6 x Steam Turbines SR geared to
    twin screws (by builder):
    24,000shp

Third of P&O's five-ship 'Strath'-class introduced in the 1930s, P&O reverted to steam turbine propulsion for the *Strathmore*, seen here departing from the Tilbury Landing Stage. Whether this change was a reflection on the performance of the turbo-electric drive installed in the initial pair is not known. The *Strathmore* also differed from the *Strathnaver* and *Strathaird* by having only a single funnel compared to their three, although the first and third were dummies. Launched on 4 April 1935, the *Strathmore* entered P&O's front-line service from London to Sydney on 26 October the same year. These duties were interrupted four years later when she became a troopship, remaining so until the winter of 1948-1949 when she was refitted for return to commercial service. Her first postwar voyage commenced on 27 October 1949. In 1961, the *Strathmore* was converted into a one-class ship for 1,200 Tourist passengers, the majority being Australian migrants. Two years later she was sold to John S Latsis of Piraeus becoming, first, the *Marianna Latsi*, then taking the name *Henrietta Latsi* in 1966. Used for pilgrim voyages and as a hotel ship at Jeddah until April 1967, she was then laid up at Eleusis prior to being broken up at La Spezia in 1969. *Mick Lindsay*

ORION

(7/1935) Orient Line
23,696grt; 665ft (202.7m) loa x
    82ft 6in (25.1m) beam
1,691 Tourist-class
Vickers-Armstrongs, Barrow-in-
    Furness
6 x Steam Turbines SR geared to
    twin screws (by builder):
    24,000shp

Contemporary with P&O's 'Strath' passenger ships were the Orient Line sisters *Orion* and *Orcades* that entered service on the London to Brisbane route on 29 September 1935 and 9 October 1937 respectively. The *Orcades* was lost in October 1942, sunk by torpedo off South Africa. Like the *Strathnaver* and *Strathaird*, the *Orion* and *Orcades* were quite revolutionary vessels compared to their predecessors, introducing vastly improved passenger amenities and featuring modern, stylish décor throughout their cabin accommodation and public rooms. They were among the very first liners to have partial air-conditioning, the first large liners to have a single mast and they introduced Orient Line's distinctive 'biscuit' hull colouring. The *Orion* spent seven years as a troopship from September 1939 after which she was refitted at Barrow to return to the Australia run from 25 February 1947. From 1958, her First-class accommodation was reduced and downgraded to Cabin standard while her Tourist-class berths were increased. In May 1960 she was included in the joint P&O-Orient Lines fleet, spending the remainder of her career as a one-class Tourist ship. Already sold for breaking-up, the *Orion* was briefly chartered in May 1963 to act as a stationary hotel ship at the Hamburg Overseas Landing Stage, as depicted here in September of that year. On completion of the charter, the *Orion* was scrapped at Tamise, Belgium. *Kenneth Wightman*

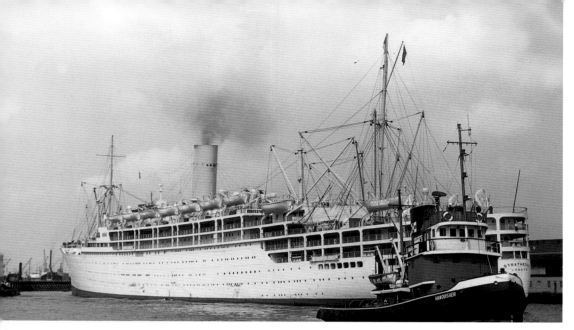

STRATHEDEN
(12/1937) P&O Line
23,732grt; 664ft 6in (202.5m) loa x 82ft 2in (25.0m) beam
527 First-class & 453 Tourist-class
Vickers-Armstrongs, Barrow-in-Furness
6 x Steam Turbines SR geared to twin screws
(by builder): 28,000shp

The *Stratheden* and *Strathallan*, the latter a war loss in December 1942, were developments of the *Strathmore* and, like her, they too were fitted with steam turbines. Completed two years after the *Strathmore*, the *Stratheden* commenced her maiden voyage on 24 December 1937, the high point of P&O's centenary year. She too became a World War 2 troopship, until 1946 when she was refitted by Vickers-Armstrongs at Newcastle. The *Stratheden* resumed the London to Sydney service in June 1947, briefly switching to the North Atlantic in 1950 when chartered for four Southampton to New York round voyages by Cunard. Like the *Strathmore*, the *Stratheden* became a Tourist-only ship in 1961 and she too was sold in 1963 to John S Latsis. Renamed *Henrietta Latsi*, for some inexplicable reason her name was changed to *Marianna Latsi* at the very time that the former *Strathmore* was being renamed in reverse. Outlasting her half-sister by two years, the *Marianna Latsi* ex *Stratheden* was broken up at La Spezia from May 1969. In the first view, tugs manoeuvre the *Stratheden* away from the Tilbury Landing Stage. The second view sees her heading towards the camera, underway outward bound. Tugs owned by the Port of London Authority, Gamecock and William Watkins are present in this dockland scene. *both Kenneth Wightman*

CANTON

(9/1938) P&O Line
16,033grt; 563ft (171.6m) loa x 73ft 4in (22.4m) beam
298 First-class & 244 Tourist-class
Alexander Stephen & Sons, Linthouse, Glasgow
6 x Steam Turbines SR geared to twin screws (by builder): 18,500shp

The last passenger ship to join P&O prior to World War 2 was the *Canton*. Ordered for the Southampton to Hong Kong service, she commenced her maiden voyage on 7 October 1938. Painted at the outset of her career in P&O's traditional colours – black hull with white line and black funnel – and the last to be so completed, her colouring became white hull and upperworks with yellow funnel on her return to commercial service after the war. In between she performed auxiliary duties, as an Armed Merchant Cruiser from November 1939 and as a troopship from 1944 to 1946. During the postwar refit by her builders, the *Canton*'s passenger accommodation was enlarged, increasing First-class numbers by 38 and Second-class, recategorised as Tourist-class, by 24. The *Canton* continued to maintain a regular schedule of sailings until August 1962 when she left London for the last time, bound for Hong Kong where she was to be broken up. The first view (right) shows her berthed alongside the Tilbury Landing Stage on 1 August 1955, while, in the second (below), the *Canton* can be seen in the King George V Dock, London, sandwiched between cargo ships of Glen Line and Shaw Savill. *both Kenneth Wightman*

ORCADES

(11/1948) Orient Line
28,399grt; 708ft 8in (216.0m)
  loa x 93ft 6in (28.5m) beam
1,635 Tourist-class
Vickers-Armstrongs, Barrow-
  in-Furness
6 x Steam Turbines DR & SR
  geared to twin screws (by
  builder): 42,500shp

Orient Line's first postwar ship was named in honour of the *Orcades* lost during the war. Costing £3.5 million, she was to be the first of a trio of similar-sized ships that upgraded the company's express service from London to Sydney, reducing the passage time from 36 to 28 days. For the first time, the Orient Line had a larger passenger liner in service than the rival P&O Line. Launched on 14 October 1947, her maiden voyage began on 14 December 1948. The *Orcades* had a distinctive design that exhibited a superstructure stepped-up towards the centre of the ship and surmounted by the bridge, placed just forward of the funnel, which had a stove-pipe extension commonly described as a 'Welsh hat'. From August 1955, the *Orcades* was redeployed on a round-the-world service to Australia, outbound via Panama and homeward-bound via Suez, extended from 1958 to include calls at San Francisco and Vancouver. The following year, she and her sisters were fully air-conditioned. After the P&O and Orient companies pooled their passenger ships in the P&O-Orient Lines subsidiary, she was refitted as a one-class ship. From 1966, when P&O acquired the balance of Orient Line's shares in the joint company, the *Orcades* became a P&O ship. Four years earlier, in anticipation it would seem, she was painted white with a yellow funnel as seen in this photograph of her near Tilbury dating from June 1965. Beyond her is one of her consorts, the *Oronsay*. Note the green boot-topping briefly retained by the Orient ships after they passed into P&O ownership. Laid up at Southampton in October 1972, the *Orcades* was broken up at Kaohsiung following her arrival there in the following February. *Kenneth Wightman*

CHUSAN

(6/1950) P&O Line

24,215grt; 672ft 6in (205.0m) loa
   x 85ft 2in (26.0m) beam

464 First-class & 541 Tourist-
   class

Vickers-Armstrongs, Barrow-in-
   Furness

6 x Steam Turbines DR & SR
   geared to twin screws (by
   builder): 42,500shp

Constructed for P&O's Far East services, the *Chusan* made her first voyage from London to Bombay on 15 September 1950, the route continuing to Japan from that November. She was in many respects a development of the prewar 'Straths', of similar tonnage and dimensions, but bearing a close resemblance to the larger and contemporaneous *Himalaya* of 1949, P&O's first postwar new building for the Australia run. She was the first large passenger ship to be fitted with Denny-Brown stabilisers. From 1951, she had a Thornycroft-type smoke deflection funnel cap installed, the like of which was fitted to the *Himalaya* two years later, and in 1959 she was air-conditioned throughout. The *Chusan*'s engines were substantially more powerful than those of the 'Strath' class, permitting a service speed of 22 knots compared with their 20 knots. From 1960, the *Chusan* inaugurated a new Orient & Pacific service that took her beyond Japan, across the Pacific to the USA with occasional calls at Australian ports. Increasingly, like her fleet-mates, she was diverted to cruising, becoming virtually dedicated to this activity by the end of her days. This view of the *Chusan* in the King George V Dock, London, shows her at a time when she was still engaged full-time on scheduled route voyages. Her career ended in June 1973 when she was broken up in Taiwan. *Kenneth Wightman*

ORONSAY
(5/1951) Orient Line

27,632grt; 708ft 8in (216.0m) loa x 93ft 6in (28.5m) beam

668 First-class & 833 Tourist-class

Vickers-Armstrongs, Barrow-in- Furness

6 x Steam Turbines DR & SR geared to twin screws (by builder): 42,500shp

Commemorating another World War 2 loss, the *Oronsay* joined the *Orcades* in Orient Line's UK to Sydney service on 16 May 1951. Broadly similar to the earlier vessel, she could be distinguished by her chunkier, plated-in mast, also the absence of the angled structure beneath her funnel, while she had fewer lifeboats suspended in davits along her boat deck. From 1958, she was placed in the trans-Pacific service operated in conjunction with P&O under the Orient & Pacific Line banner. This added calls at Los Angeles on the return voyage to the UK. In 1960 the *Oronsay* was absorbed into the joint P&O-Orient Lines fleet and six years later she became a wholly-owned P&O ship, as explained under the *Orcades*. The *Oronsay*, repainted white with a yellow funnel, served under the P&O house flag for another nine years, spending an increasing amount of time on luxury cruises. She was scrapped at Kaohsiung, arriving there at the end of her final voyage on 7 October 1975. The photograph of her in Tilbury Docks (top left) shows her original Orient Line livery, while the second (left) view, taken in September 1971, shows her departing Southampton as a P&O vessel, after adaptation into a one-class ship for approximately 1,500 in Tourist-class. *Kenneth Wightman & Mick Lindsay*

ORSOVA
(3/1954) Orient Line
28,870grt; 722ft 10in (220.3m) loa x 90ft 7in (27.6m) beam
681 First-class & 813 Tourist-class
Vickers-Armstrongs, Barrow-in-Furness
6 x Steam Turbines DR & SR geared to twin screws (by builder): 42,500shp

Last of Orient Line's three ships built under its war-loss replacement and fleet enhancement programme was the £6.5 million *Orsova*. While she retained a similar look overall to the *Orcades* and *Oronsay*, she deviated from the earlier pair in certain detailed respects, and was more a contemporary of P&O's *Arcadia* and *Iberia*. She had a longer, narrower hull, her funnel was tapered at the rear and, unusually, she did not have a mast – the first ocean liner to lack this feature. She joined the *Orcades* and *Oronsay* in the Antipodes service in 1954, making her maiden departure from London on 17 March of that year. Where the *Oronsay*'s route was extended from 1958 to include a call at Los Angeles, likewise the *Orsova* worked the Orient & Pacific Line service, calling at San Francisco while homeward bound to the UK. The *Orsova*'s subsequent career followed along the lines of her fleet partners and, in February 1974, having spent much of her remaining years as a P&O cruise ship, she was disposed of for scrap, broken up at Kaohsiung. The photographs show two phases in the life of the *Orsova*, first as the Orient Line flagship in the late 1950s (right) and, in the second view (below), taken in September 1973, during a P&O cruise to Tenerife. *both Mick Lindsay*

ARCADIA
(2/1954) P&O Line
29,734grt; 721ft 4in (219.9m) loa
  x 90ft 8in (27.6m) beam
675 First-class & 735 Tourist-class
John Brown & Co, Clydebank
6 x Steam Turbines DR & SR
  geared to twin screws (by
  builder): 42,500shp

After World War 2, P&O reinstated its Australia services with the renovated *Maloja* and *Mooltan*, *Strathnaver*, *Strathaird*, *Strathmore* and *Stratheden*, supplemented from 1949 with the new, well-appointed *Himalaya*. However, in the face of Orient Line's fleet improvements, P&O were obliged to hasten their own fleet upgrade plans, centred on the drive to reduce the passage time of the Australia mail service to 28 days. The outcome of this took the form of the sister liners *Arcadia* and *Iberia*, the first of the pair built on Clydebank (birthplace of Cunard's *Queens*), the second at Belfast. P&O's three-ship operation, using the *Himalaya*, *Arcadia* and *Iberia* – each capable of 22 knots service speed – working in conjunction with Orient Line's express ships, permitted twice-monthly sailings from London and Sydney. All were switched to the trans-Pacific service from the late 1950s. As her career unfolded, the *Arcadia* was diverted more and more often to cruising, ultimately becoming a dedicated cruise ship in 1973, making excursions from Californian ports to Alaska or Mexico. She was finally sold for breaking-up at Taiwan in February 1979. In this study of the *Arcadia*, taken in July 1968, she is berthed at the P&O Passenger Terminal in Southampton's Western Docks. *Mick Lindsay*

IBERIA
(9/1954) P&O Line
29,614grt; 718ft 8in (219.1m) loa
   x 90ft 10in (27.7m) beam
673 First-class & 733 Tourist-class
Harland & Wolff, Belfast
6 x Steam Turbines DR & SR
   geared to twin screws (by
   builder): 42,500shp

Photographed off Gravesend being assisted by two London tugs, the *Iberia* joined her consort *Arcadia* on the Australia service from Tilbury on 28 September 1954. The only distinction between them was the styling of their funnels – the *Arcadia*'s, which was more tapered, had a black domed cap while the *Iberia*'s, which was all yellow, had a grill at the front top. During a major refit in 1961 she was air-conditioned throughout and had stabilisers installed. The *Arcadia* had been adapted in like fashion during her 1959 refit. The *Iberia*'s career followed a similar path to that of the *Arcadia* until it culminated in her early retirement in September 1972. P&O prematurely disposed of the *Iberia*, after just 18 years of service, because she had a higher fuel consumption, a matter of vital commercial importance during the oil crisis of the early 1970s. It is likely, too, that, as passenger travel by sea declined, the equally competitive cruise trade could only support so many vessels. Also it was expensive and far from ideal to convert liners, whose accommodation was laid out for more than one grade of occupancy, for a quite different role where passenger expectations were in complete variance. When fleet cutbacks became unavoidable, P&O sacrificed the less profitable *Iberia* while her slightly older sister *Arcadia* was retained.
Kenneth Wightman

CATHAY
(10/1957) ex *Baudouinville* (1961) P&O
  Line
13,809grt; 557ft 9in (170.0m) loa x 70ft
  1in (21.3m) beam
231 one-class
Soc. Anon. Cockerill-Ougrée, Hoboken,
  Belgium
2 x Steam Turbines DR geared to single
  screw (by builder at Seraing): 12,500shp

When the old *Corfu* and *Carthage* were retired, P&O purchased the Cie. Maritime Belge sister ships *Jadotville* and *Baudouinville* as replacements. The former became the *Chitral*, the latter the *Cathay*. After the pair had been overhauled and refitted to meet P&O's requirements, they entered service from London to Yokohama in March and April 1961 respectively. The *Cathay* was photographed in an unknown location, probably the River Thames, in April 1964. In 1970, the pair were transferred to the ownership of the Eastern & Australian Steamship Co, spending the next six years sailing between Far East ports and Australia. This ended with the sale of the *Chitral* for breaking up. The *Cathay*, in contrast was reprieved, sold to the People's Republic of China in January 1976 as a training ship for mercantile marine officers under the name *Kangshin*. Renamed *Shanghai* in 1978, she then worked a coastal route from Shanghai via other Chinese ports to Hong Kong. She was still in service in 1984, registered with the Shanghai Hai Xing Shipping Co. *Kenneth Wightman*

ORIANA

(12/1960) P&O Line

41,915grt; 804ft (245.1m) loa x 97ft 2in (29.6m) beam

638 First-class & 1,496 Tourist-class

Vickers-Armstrongs, Barrow-in-Furness

6 x Steam Turbines DR geared to twin screws (by builder): 80,000shp

Ironically, what in retrospect was Orient Line's zenith was also its swan song. Taking the form of the *Oriana*, she was one of two spectacular new passenger ships introduced to the Australia passenger service at a time when, equally ironically, it was fast reaching its peak and would soon be in decline. It could be argued that the *Oriana* was never purely an Orient ship, despite first donning that company's colours, because, on her entry into service on 3 December 1960, she immediately became part of the P&O-Orient Lines' combined fleet. Within six years, the Orient Line was but a fading memory while the *Oriana*, along with the *Canberra*, continued to make regular P&O sailings to Sydney from a new UK base at Southampton for another seven seasons. During their all too brief sojourn on the Australia run, the *Oriana* and *Canberra* elevated passenger standards to an all-time high. Furnishings and fittings were vastly improved, they were air-conditioned throughout and had stabilisers to reduce rolling. Their much larger power plants gave them a service speed of 27½ knots, allowing the completion of the passage in 24 days, well over a week less than it had taken when the 'Strath' quintet had been the company's front line ships, themselves considered fast ships in their day. The *Oriana* had four athwartships manoeuvring propellers, two forwards and two aft. By the mid-1970s, just three former scheduled-service ships remained in the P&O fleet, being the *Arcadia*, *Oriana* and *Canberra*, all three employed as cruise ships. The *Oriana* was ultimately sold out of P&O ownership in 1986, traded to the Daiwa Group to become a static cultural & tourist attraction in Beppu Bay, Kyushu, Japan. She remained there until 1995 when she was re-sold for a similar role at Qinquangdau in China, being repositioned in the River Huangpo at Shanghai from 1998. A slow process of refurbishment was expected to result in the *Oriana* returning to some sort of active service – but it was not to be. Moved to Dalian in 2002, the *Oriana* was overwhelmed by a typhoon on 18 June 2004 and capsized. Though righted, further expense to restore the 45-year old liner could not be justified and instead the *Oriana* was demolished in India in 2005. The photograph shows the *Oriana* in happier times, at Southampton on 16 July 1977, four years after she had made her last route voyage to Australia. *Mick Lindsay*

CANBERRA

(6/1961) P&O Line
45,733grt; 818ft 6in (249.5m) loa
    x 102ft 6in (31.2m) beam
548 First-class & 1,650 Tourist-
    class
Harland & Wolff, Belfast
Turbo-electric, comprising
    2 steam turbines (by builder),
    connected to electric generators
    and motors, by Associated
    Electrical Industries, Rugby,
    driving twin screws: 85,000shp

Like Orient Line's *Oriana*, P&O Line's *Canberra* represented the peak of the company's long development of the express mail liner for the Australia route, becoming, on her entry into service, the largest passenger liner ever built for the Australia service. Interestingly, each Line's approach had resulted in a quite different solution but both were marvellous, exceptional engineering achievements. In the *Canberra*, P&O opted to return to turbo-electric drive, not used since the *Strathnaver* and *Strathaird* of the early 1930s. Externally, she had a radically different design, with her engines and twin athwartships funnels placed aft, freeing-up vast uninterrupted areas of deck space forward, which were modelled for the maximum benefit and pleasure of her passengers. Other features of the *Canberra* included full air-conditioning, fin stabilisers and directional thrust propellers in the forward part of her underwater hull. The *Canberra* began her maiden voyage on 2 June 1961. Thereafter, she and the *Oriana* maintained a joint round-the-world service taking them from Southampton to Sydney and Auckland, returning to Southampton across the Pacific, via US West Coast ports, the Panama Canal and Atlantic. No longer able to compete with the airlines, P&O abandoned this service in 1973 and the *Canberra* was sent cruising full-time, an activity interrupted only by her brief but acclaimed participation in the task force sent to recover the Falkland Islands from Argentine forces in April 1982. Returned to her owners that July, the *Canberra* completed another 15 years as a cruise ship, attracting a loyal following. She had out-survived the *Oriana*'s active career by a decade but, sold for scrapping at Gadani Beach, Pakistan in October 1997, she did not out-live her former consort, which was still in existence eight years later. This dramatic view, taken following a storm, shows the *Canberra* with the Southampton tug *Totland*. *Mick Lindsay*

HIGHLAND MONARCH
(10/1928) Royal Mail Lines
14,216grt; 544ft 6in (165.9m) loa x
    69ft 2in (21.1m) beam
104 First-class & 335 Third-class
Harland & Wolff, Belfast
2 x Oil 4DA 8-cyl Burmeister & Wain
    (by builder): 10,000bhp

Lead ship of a six-ship class ordered by the Nelson Line in the 1920s for the River Plate service from London, the *Highland Monarch* made her maiden departure on 18 October 1928. The group were a further example of the many Pirrie-Kylsant motorships constructed by Harland & Wolff at Belfast in this period. Others were delivered to Royal Mail Line, Union-Castle and the White Star Line. Royal Mail Line absorbed the Nelson Line and its fleet in 1932 but, apart from a change of livery, this had little impact on the ships or their service. World War 2 trooping by the *Highland Monarch* continued until 1946 when she was reconditioned by her builders for return to the London to Buenos Aires route. The *Highland Monarch* was broken up at Dalmuir from 28 April 1960. She was the last survivor of the 'Highland' class still operating under the Red Ensign. The photograph shows her at the Tilbury Landing Stage. *Kenneth Wightman*

ANDES

(12/1939) Royal Mail Lines
25,895grt; 669ft 4in (204.0m) loa
    x 83ft 6in (25.5m) beam
480 one-class
Harland & Wolff, Belfast
6 x Steam Turbines SR geared to
    twin screws (by builder):
    30,000shp

The *Andes* was the last British passenger liner to be constructed prior to the outbreak of World War 2 but she did not commence civilian employment for almost nine years. Her maiden voyage to Montevideo and Buenos Aires, scheduled to commence on 26 September 1939, was cancelled and the *Andes* was sent instead to Halifax, Nova Scotia for conversion into a troopship, sailing there on 9 December. The *Andes'* long years of auxiliary service concluded with an emotionally-charged task, to bring the first child evacuees of the Children's Overseas Reception Board (CORB) programme back home to the UK in 1946. Released from Government service in 1947 and given a thorough refit, the *Andes* finally started her maiden commercial voyage from Southampton on 22 January 1948. Eleven years on the 'La Plata' service ensued but, as it became increasingly difficult to fill her 607 berths (403 First-class & 204 Second-class), a new role was conceived for the *Andes*. In November 1959, she went to the 'De Schelde' shipyard at Vlissingen where, over the next six months, she was rebuilt as a cruise ship with reduced passenger accommodation in a single class. Befitting her new purpose, her previously black hull was over-painted white. On 10 June 1960, she commenced her maiden cruise voyage from Southampton, launching a second eleven-year phase of her life. Despite being among the very first of the large passenger liners transferred to the cruise business, she could not compete with the purpose-built cruise ships that began to appear in the early 1970s. So, in May 1971, she was paid off for disposal and broken up at Ghent in Belgium. *Mick Lindsay*

ARLANZA

(9/1960) Royal Mail Lines
20,362grt; 584ft (178.0m) loa
x 78ft 3in (23.8m) beam
107 First-class, 82 Cabin-class
& 275 Third-class
Harland & Wolff, Belfast
2 x Oil 2SA 6-cyl (by builder):
20,000bhp

Last of three passenger-cargo liners ordered for the London to Buenos Aires service, the *Arlanza* and her sisters had passenger accommodation for 464 in three classes, an operationally expensive arrangement for the time, and a refrigerated cargo capacity of 435,000ft^3. Having withdrawn the *Andes* from this very route barely a year earlier, it is hard to understand where, with declining meat shipments and passenger traffic on this trade route, three such vessels were to find sufficient passengers or cargo to be viable. It has been remarked that the decision to build them at all remains a mystery of corporate planning. Bearing this out, they served Royal Mail for barely nine years and were then sold as a trio to Shaw Savill & Albion in 1969, the *Arlanza* becoming the *Arawa*. Placed on the Southampton to Australia and New Zealand route, Shaw Savill's acquisition of these vessels was equally curious for they were to only find employment for the next two years. Sold again in 1971, this final transaction proved a more worthwhile proposition, as the three ships were acquired for conversion into car carriers, a function they continued to perform for ten years. The *Arawa* was purchased by Hoegh Ugland Autoliners and renamed *Hoegh Transit*. Further name changes followed: *Hoegh Trotter* (1972), *Hual Trotter* (1980) and finally *Trotter* (1980). She was broken up at Kaohsiung from December 1981. The *Arlanza*, shown in her original guise, was photographed in the London Docks in June 1966. *Kenneth Wightman*

TAMAROA

(2/1922) ex *Sophocles* (1926)
   Shaw Savill & Albion
12,375grt; 518ft 9in (158.1m) loa x
   63ft 2in (19.3m) beam
372 Tourist-class
Harland & Wolff, Belfast
4 x Steam Turbines DR geared to
   twin screws (by builder):
   6,750shp

The *Tamaroa* and her sister *Mataroa* were passenger-cargo liners built originally for the Aberdeen Line, entering service as the *Sophocles* and *Diogenes* respectively. Initially chartered by Shaw Savill from 1926 when they were renamed, they transferred fully to that company's ownership in 1932. Built as coal-burners, their new owners had them immediately converted to oil firing. As built, the pair carried 131 First-class and 422 Third-class passengers. Postwar, following troopship service, their passenger accommodation was adapted into a single class, concentrating on the emigrant traffic to New Zealand. By the time the photograph of the *Tamaroa* in the Royal Albert Dock was taken, she and the *Mataroa* were nearing the end of their days. Seriously dated by the mid-1950s in respect of their passenger amenities, even allowing for the austere standards of Tourist-class at that time, besides having limited cargo carrying value, the *Tamaroa* and her sister survived only to March 1957. They were sold for breaking up, in the case of the *Tamaroa* at Blyth, Northumberland. *Kenneth Wightman*

DOMINION MONARCH

(1/1939) Shaw Savill & Albion
26,463grt; 682ft 1in (207.8m) loa
  x 84ft 10in (25.9m) beam
508 First-class
Swan, Hunter & Wigham
  Richardson, Wallsend-on-Tyne
4 x Oil 2SA 5-cyl Doxford (2 by
  builder & 2 by William
  Doxford, Sunderland):
  32,000bhp

This wonderful study of the motor passenger liner *Dominion Monarch* shows her in the King George V Dock, at a time when London's Royal Docks Group was a veritable 'City of Ships'. Aft of the *Dominion Monarch* can be seen one of Royal Mail's 'Highland' class motorships. The *Dominion Monarch* was a unique and distinctive passenger ship, conceived as a hybrid vessel and provided with a total cargo capacity of 659,000ft^3, equal to that of the largest pure cargo ships of her day, along with substantial passenger accommodation, permitting her to derive revenue for her owners from two sources. Her two-island design set her aside from all other contemporary passenger-carrying vessels and this, with her size and her two motorship funnels, made her instantly recognisable. She had hardly got into her stride, making her maiden voyage from London to Wellington on 17 February 1939, when she was commandeered for troopship service on the outbreak of World War 2. She had a narrow escape in January 1942, at the time of the fall of Singapore, when she was trapped in dry-dock as Japanese forces threatened to take the island. Escape was made possible by the intervention of her own crew who flooded the dock to release the ship. Trooping duties ended in July 1947 but, following a refit, she returned to the Wellington service in 1948. She maintained this service for the next 14 years but the *Dominion Monarch*'s unique trade was gradually dwindling such that by the early 1960s she became surplus to her owners' requirements. Sold for breaking up, she was briefly chartered as a hotel ship at the Seattle World's Fair in 1962 before heading to the scrapyard at Osaka under the name *Dominion Monarch Maru*. Kenneth Wightman

SOUTHERN CROSS

(3/1955) Shaw Savill & Albion
20,204grt; 603ft 10in (184.0m) loa
  x 78ft 6in (23.9m) beam
1,160 Tourist-class
Harland & Wolff, Belfast
4 x Steam Turbines DR geared to
  twin screws (by builder):
  20,000shp

Shaw Savill & Albion had built up a prosperous shipping business centred primarily on the cargo trade. Even such large passenger liners as the *Ceramic* of 1913 and the *Dominion Monarch* had vast hold capacities for the conveyance of refrigerated and general produce. It came as something of a surprise, therefore, when Shaw Savill introduced the revolutionary, passenger-only *Southern Cross* on a round-the-world service from Southampton, commencing 29 March 1955. Her engines-aft configuration was equally radical; reprising a design concept pioneered in the Matson Line steamers *Lurline*, *Wilhelmina* and *Maui*, back in the years either side of World War 1. Although the *Southern Cross* was switched to cruising from June 1971, having continued for 16 years with her unique four voyages a year, scheduled service role, her fortunes with Shaw Savill declined. She was laid up, first at Southampton and then in the River Fal until, in January 1973, she was sold to Cia de Vap Cerulea SA, Ithaka. Modernised internally she became the cruise ship *Calypso*, based at Piraeus. Although she changed owners and names several more times over the next 32 years: *Calypso I* (1980), *Azure Seas* (1980) *Ocean Breeze* (1992), the old liner remained a firm favourite, both popular with her passengers and financially successful, surviving until 2003 when she was finally broken up in Bangladesh. *Mick Lindsay*

NORTHERN STAR

(6/1962) Shaw Savill & Albion

24,731grt; 650ft (198.1m) loa x 83ft
8in (25.5m) beam

1,412 Tourist-class

Vickers-Armstrongs, Newcastle

4 x Steam Turbines DR geared to twin
screws by Parsons Marine Turbine
Co, Wallsend-on-Tyne: 22,000shp

Arising from the extraordinary success of the *Southern Cross*'s round-the-world passenger operation, Shaw Savill elected to provide her with a consort, the *Northern Star*, which made her maiden voyage from Southampton on 10 July 1962. Despite following the same formula, inexplicably the *Northern Star* was not as successful a ship, her inferior performance contrasting with her older partner's conspicuous achievement. The result was an extremely short life span, ending in December 1974 when, at just 12 years of age, she went to the breakers yard at Kaohsiung. It was indeed a sad and premature farewell for a liner that, in truth, was most elegant. With her taller, slimmer funnel she had a more attractive profile than the *Southern Cross*. The photograph below, taken in November 1971, shows the *Northern Star* as she steams out of the River Itchen at Southampton with the Red Funnel tug *Dunnose* in attendance, bound for South Africa. *Mick Lindsay*

ARANDA

(4/1960) ex *Aragon* (1969) Shaw Savill
   & Albion
18,575grt; 584ft (178.0m) loa x 78ft 3in
   (23.8m) beam
464 one-class
Harland & Wolff, Belfast
2 x Oil 2SA 6-cyl (by builder): 20,000bhp

The *Aragon* joined Shaw Savill in 1969 and, renamed *Aranda*, she served for two years in the Southampton to Australia and New Zealand service. Her sisters were transferred as part of the same deal. The three ships of the class had a distinctive, two-island superstructure configuration reminiscent of that of Shaw Savill's *Dominion Monarch* retired in 1962. The *Aranda* and her sisters, *Akaroa* ex *Amazon* and *Arawa* ex *Arlanza*, were sold out of the Shaw Savill fleet after just two years, in 1971, all being subsequently converted into car carriers. The *Aranda*, purchased by Hoegh Ugland Autoliners, was rebuilt at Rijeka as the *Hoegh Traveller*, renamed *Traveller* in 1980. A year later, in October 1981, she was scrapped in Taiwan. *CCQ*

ARUNDEL CASTLE

(4/1921) Union-Castle Line
19,206grt; 686ft 3in (209.2m) loa x 72ft 6in (22.1m) beam
169 First-class & 371 Tourist-class
Harland & Wolff, Belfast
6 x Steam Turbines SR geared to twin screw (by builder): 15,000shp

The *Arundel Castle* and her Clyde-built sister *Windsor Castle* were the last four-funnelled liners to be built. When she made her maiden voyage from Southampton to Cape Town on 22 April 1922, the *Arundel Castle* was the first mail steamer to enter service with Union-Castle after the company became part of Lord Kylsant's Royal Mail Group. Laid down in 1915, the name *Amroth Castle* had been originally intended for her. However, World War I intervened, delaying her construction, and when launched on 11 September 1919 she was christened instead as the *Arundel Castle*. The new mail contract to South Africa called for a 13½-day passage, taking three days off the old schedule. To achieve this, in 1937 she became the first of five mail ships to be refitted with higher-powered machinery by Harland & Wolff and in the course of the conversion she was lengthened with a new bow – her original length had been 630ft 6in (192.2m) – and given two sleek funnels in place of the four she had been completed with. During World War 2 the *Arundel Castle* served as a troopship, steaming some half a million miles, and was engaged in the North African and Sicilian landings. She remained on Government service long after the end of the war, being engaged as an emigrant ship to South Africa, and she did not receive a major overhaul and refit by her builders until 1949. She finally resumed the Cape mail run in September 1950 with her accommodation rearranged for two classes – before World War 2 there had been three classes and, when new, four. In December 1958 she made her last voyage from Southampton to Cape Town and continued on to Kowloon for scrapping in 1959. The photograph shows the *Arundel Castle* in the Solent en route for South Africa in 1957, having left Southampton on Thursday at 4pm, Union-Castle's clockwork-regular departure day and time. *Mick Lindsay*

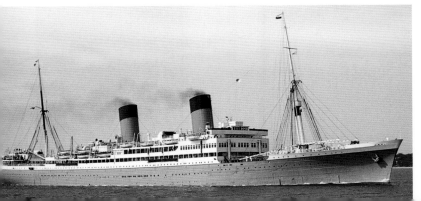

CARNARVON CASTLE

(6/1926) Union-Castle Line
20,148grt; 686ft 3in (209.2m) loa x 73ft 6in (22.4m) beam
216 First-class & 401 Tourist-class
Harland & Wolff, Belfast
2 x Oil 2DA 10-cyl Burmeister & Wain (by builder): 15,000bhp

Originally built with two squat funnels, a style that was to become a Harland & Wolff trademark, the *Carnarvon Castle* was Union-Castle's first motor ship and its first liner to exceed 20,000 gross tons. She entered service on the Southampton to Cape Town service on 16 July 1926. Between 1937 and 1938 she was refitted along with four other mail ships, three of them having new B&W higher-powered diesels installed to increase their speed to meet the new mail contract requirements. Simultaneously, she was lengthened and her original two funnels were substituted by a single one of squat profile. On 9 October 1939 she was taken up as an Armed Merchant Cruiser and as such had her original foremast and most of her lifeboats removed. In this role, on 5 December 1940, she engaged with and damaged the German surface raider *Thor* in the South Atlantic. The *Carnarvon Castle* was herself hit and headed for Montevideo for repairs. In 1944 she was fitted out as a troopship at New York and not released from this role until March 1947. Before resuming the Cape Run on 15 June 1950, she was given a major refit by her builders. After 36 years service she was withdrawn in 1962 and arrived at Mihara, Japan on 8 September for demolition. This view shows a full broadside elevation of the *Carnarvon Castle* moored in Southampton's Western Docks. In addition to her passenger accommodation, she had a cargo capacity of 507,747ft³, including 207,759ft³ refrigerated space. Her sleek lines belie the fact that she was built in 1926. *Mick Lindsay*

STIRLING CASTLE

(1/1936) Union-Castle Line

25,554grt; 725ft (221.0m) loa x
82ft 6in (25.1m) beam

245 First-class & 538 Tourist-class

Harland & Wolff, Belfast

2 x Oil 2DA 10-cyl Burmeister &
Wain (by builder): 24,000bhp

Following on from the earlier, pioneering Union-Castle motor ships such as the *Carnarvon*, *Winchester* and *Warwick Castles*, the next generation of vessels to satisfy the mail contract criteria was spearheaded by the *Stirling* and *Athlone Castles*. The *Stirling Castle* sailed on her maiden voyage on 7 February 1936, and later that year, on 21 August, she made a record run of 13 days 9 hours from Southampton to Cape Town. She was used as a troopship from 1940 onwards and in this wartime capacity sailed over 500,000 miles conveying some 128,000 persons. Like her sister, she was employed mainly on the North Atlantic from 1943 transporting American troops to the UK and on one eastbound crossing she carried over 6,000 G,I's. In 1946, following her release from Government service, she returned to her builders for a major overhaul, eventually returning to service in 1947. The *Stirling Castle* arrived back in Southampton on 30 November 1965 at the end of her last voyage from the Cape, before being put up for disposal. She arrived at Mihira, Japan, on 3 March 1966, to be broken up. In this port stern quarter view the *Stirling Castle* is seen departing from Southampton, ably assisted by four Red Funnel tugs. *CCQ*

ATHLONE CASTLE

(5/1936) Union-Castle Line
25,567grt; 725ft (221.0m) loa x
   82ft 6in (25.1m) beam
245 First-class & 538 Tourist-class
Harland & Wolff, Belfast
2 x Oil 2DA 10-cyl Burmeister &
   Wain (by builder): 24,000bhp

The *Athlone Castle* was launched by Princess Alice, Countess of Athlone on 28 November 1935. She was a sister ship to the *Stirling Castle* and similar to the later and larger *Capetown Castle*. She departed on her maiden voyage on 22 May 1936 and in December 1938 inaugurated a slightly more accelerated service to South Africa. Her original accommodation layout provided for 719 passengers in two classes. From 1939 she was taken up as a troopship and from 1943 onwards was employed principally on the North Atlantic transporting US troops to Britain. In 1946 the *Athlone Castle* was released from Government service and returned to her builders for a major refit, resuming the Southampton to Cape Town service in 1947. After 30 years' service, she arrived at Kaohsiung on 13 September 1965, for scrapping. This three-quarter stern view of her in Southampton's Western Docks shows the *Athlone Castle*'s cruiser stern to its fullest advantage. It has been recorded that the *Athlone Castle* and the *Stirling Castle* were widely regarded as two of the most handsome motor liners ever built, a view borne out by this and the previous photograph. *Kenneth Wightman*

EDINBURGH CASTLE

(11/1948) Union-Castle Line
28,705grt; 747ft 5in (227.8m) loa
  x 84ft (25.6m) beam
214 First-class & 541 Tourist-class
Harland & Wolff, Belfast
6 Steam Turbines DR geared to
  twin screws (by builder):
  35,000shp

As a healthy postwar order for Harland & Wolff, the *Edinburgh Castle* along with her sister *Pretoria Castle* were built as replacements for the wartime losses *Warwick Castle* and *Windsor Castle*. When she was launched on 16 October 1947, it was the late Princess Margaret who performed the christening ceremony. The *Edinburgh Castle* was the company's first steamship after 20 years' commitment to motor propulsion, reverting to the six steam turbine arrangement. She entered the Southampton to Durban service on 9 December 1948. As built she had two masts and seven holds for cargo, served by derricks of 3, 5, 10 and 30 tons lifting capacity. In 1967 she underwent a major refit in which her interiors were modernised and her mainmast was removed, replaced by a signalling mast atop the bridge. After 27 years' service, her last voyage to Durban began on 5 March 1976, after which she made a single voyage without passengers. She was sold in May 1976 and arrived at Kaohsiung a month later for breaking up. This was just one year prior to Union-Castle's complete abandonment of its service to South Africa. This fine picture of the *Edinburgh Castle*, alongside Southampton's Western Docks, shows off the sparkling paintwork of her lavender hull. *Mick Lindsay*

RHODESIA CASTLE
(11/1951) Union-Castle Line
17,041grt; 576ft 6in (175.7m) loa
x 74ft 5in (22.7m) beam
526 Cabin-class
Harland & Wolff, Belfast
6 Steam Turbines DR geared to
twin screws (by builder):
14,400shp

The *Rhodesia Castle*, launched on 5 April 1951, was the first of a trio of liners for Union-Castle's round-Africa service, the other two being the *Kenya Castle* and *Braemar Castle*. Handing over of the latter, late in 1952, marked the completion of Union-Castle's postwar liner replacement programme. The *Rhodesia Castle* sailed on her maiden voyage from London on 18 October 1951. She sailed out via Suez and down the East coast of Africa and around the Cape (clockwise), as did the *Kenya Castle*, whereas the *Braemar Castle* circumnavigated in the opposite direction. Passengers in a single-class were afforded a luxurious standard of accommodation. During a refit in 1960-1961, the *Rhodesia Castle* had her funnel heightened by the addition of a dome top, making her look rather more modern. The trio operated a successful service for colonials and 'expats' alike while it lasted but, just as experienced by British India's *Kenya* and *Uganda*, it was undermined by 'Uhuru' in Kenya, UDI in Rhodesia and the Beira Patrol. The final death-blow was closure of the Suez Canal following the Six-Day War in 1967. In May that year the *Rhodesia Castle* was laid up in the River Blackwater and on 26 October 1967 she arrived at Kaohsiung for demolition. This rare photograph of the *Rhodesia Castle*, taken at Kilindini, Kenya between 1962 and 1965, shows her with domed funnel extension. This port was run by the East African Railways and benefited from having fairly modern dock-handling facilities available for cargo handling. Note the ship's pronounced cruiser stern, a Harland & Wolff hallmark since the 1920s. *Mick Lindsay*

REINA DEL MAR
(4/1956) Union-Castle Line
20,750grt
1,047 one-class
for other details, see the *Reina del Mar* under Pacific Steam Navigation Co

A downturn in the South American passenger trade led to the eight-year-old *Reina del Mar* being refitted into a one-class cruise ship in 1964. She re-entered service in June of that year under Union-Castle management and five months later she was painted in Union-Castle livery. She was employed solely for cruising, from Southampton during the summer months and from Cape Town in the winter. During her cruising era, from 1964 to 1974, it is reputed that she was one of the most successful cruise ships of the day, but rising fuel prices in the 1970s made her economically unviable. She had been transferred from Pacific Steam Navigation to Royal Mail Lines ownership in 1969 and, despite her increasing operational costs, in September 1973 she was sold outright to Union-Castle, which had remained her managers throughout. Less than two years later, on 30 July 1975 and after only 19 years' service, she arrived at Kaohsiung for scrapping. This shot of the *Reina del Mar*, fully decked out in bunting, shows her departing on her last cruise from Southampton on 26 October 1974. *Mick Lindsay*

PENDENNIS CASTLE
(11/1958) Union-Castle Line
28,453grt; 763ft 3in (232.6m) loa
x 83ft 10in (25.5m) beam
197 First-class & 473 Tourist-class
Harland & Wolff, Belfast
4 SteamTurbines DR geared to
twin screws (by builder):
46,000shp

Launched on 10 December 1957, the *Pendennis Castle* was the first Union-Castle liner to be fitted with stabilisers. This feature was incorporated late on in her construction, requiring a 15ft increase in her designed hull length in order to accommodate them. A break from tradition was her tapered funnel and curved, raked stem but she still retained the distinctive Harland & Wolff cruiser stern. She was the first of the company's liners to be fitted with a bridge console that extended the full width of the wheelhouse. She made her maiden voyage from Southampton to Durban on 1 January 1959, replacing the 38-year-old *Arundel Castle* that had been withdrawn a month earlier. In February 1968 she made a fast run from Cape Town to Southampton in 10 days 15 hours and 12 minutes. After only 17 years on the mail and passenger service she made her last return voyage from South Africa on 27 May 1976 and the following August she was sold to Ocean Queen Navigation Corp of Panama and renamed *Ocean Queen*. She was laid up in Hong Kong and sold on again in 1977 as the *Sinbad*, a name later modified to *Sinbad I*. She never sailed again and arrived at Kaohsiung during April 1980 for scrapping. This photograph shows the refined lines of the *Pendennis Castle*, as she steams down Southampton Water on a June afternoon in 1971 en route to the Cape. *Mick Lindsay*

WINDSOR CASTLE
(7/1960) Union-Castle Line
37,647grt; 783ft 1in (238.7m)
   loa x 92ft 6in (28.2m) beam
191 First-class & 591 Tourist-
   class
Cammell Laird & Co,
   Birkenhead
4 Steam Turbines DR geared to
   twin screws (by builder):
   49,000shp

When launched on 23 June 1959, by Queen Elizabeth the Queen Mother, the *Windsor Castle* became both the largest liner owned by Union-Castle and the largest passenger ship ever to be built by Cammell Laird. At the time she was also the largest passenger vessel to be constructed in a British yard since the *Queen Elizabeth* of 1940. Her accommodation for just under 800 passengers was fully air-conditioned and she was stabilised. She was an imposing ship with a high, built-up central superstructure, distinguishing her from earlier Union-Castle liners. She sailed on her maiden voyage on 18 August 1960, a week after the liner that she was replacing, the *Winchester Castle*, had sailed on her last trip. The *Windsor Castle* soon established herself as the flagship of the newly formed British & Commonwealth Shipping Co. Besides her passenger complement, she also had refrigerated cargo capacity for 352,000ft^3 of fruit and perishable goods as well as 271,000ft^3 hold capacity for general cargo. The *Windsor Castle* left Southampton on 12 August 1977 on her 124th and final voyage to the Cape, marking the company's closure of the South African mail service after 120 years. Upon her return she was sold to John S Latsis of Piraeus and departed Southampton on 3 October for Greece as the *Margarita L*. In Piraeus she was converted into a luxury accommodation vessel stationed at Jeddah in Saudi Arabia. Later, after she had been towed from her jetty at Jeddah back to Greece for lay-up at Eleusis, she was offered for sale in 1998. Sailing under the name *Rita*, she arrived at Alang, India in August 2005 for demolition. This view shows the *Windsor Castle* returning to Southampton from South Africa in August 1975, with Red Funnel's *Culver* at her bows. *Mick Lindsay*

TRANSVAAL CASTLE
(12/1961) Union-Castle Line
32,697grt; 760ft 2in (231.7m)
  loa x 90ft 2in (27.5m) beam
728 one-class
John Brown & Co, Clydebank
4 Steam Turbines DR geared to
  twin screws (by builder):
  44,000shp

When the *Transvaal Castle* was launched on 17 January 1961 she was the fifth new passenger vessel to enter the Cape mail service since the War but also the last. She was the first Union-Castle ship to be built with a bulbous bow and she offered a single 'Hotel class' of accommodation for her entire passenger complement. In another change from her predecessors, she was the first liner to employ women as 'stewardettes' as opposed to waitresses. Her maiden voyage from Southampton to Durban commenced on 18 January 1962. On 12 January 1966, the *Transvaal Castle* was transferred to the South African Marine Corp and renamed *S.A. Vaal*. As such, she was painted all-white with a change of funnel livery. Besides carrying passengers, the *S.A. Vaal* was later, in the mid-1960s, fitted with wine tanks for the carriage of bulk imports of South African sherry to the UK. In February 1969 she was re-registered at Cape Town. Following the closure of the South African mail and passenger service, the *S.A. Vaal* was withdrawn and sold to Carnival Cruises of Miami. Renamed *Festivale*, she was overhauled for cruising and began a second career with her new company in consort with a number of other ex-British liners. Acquired in 1996 by Premier Cruises and renamed *Island Breeze* for charter, her owners renamed her *Big Red Boat III* in 2000 as part of a corporate rebranding exercise. Within nine months the company had collapsed financially and creditors seized the ship, which by then was idle. On 9 July 2003 as the *Big Boat*, she arrived at Alang, India, for demolition. This photograph of the *Transvaal Castle* shows her arriving at Southampton. Although the photo is undated, judging by the superb condition of her paintwork and the scaffolding around her mast, it could well be her delivery voyage from the builders in January 1962. *Mick Lindsay*

Front cover:
MAURETANIA
(6/1939) Cunard Line
35,655grt; 771ft 10in (235.2m) loa x 89ft 5in (27.2m) beam
475 First-class, 390 Cabin-class & 300 Tourist-class
Cammell Laird & Co, Birkenhead
6 Steam Turbines SR geared to twin screws (by builder): 42,000shp

When launched on 28 July 1938, the *Mauretania* perpetuated the name of one of the most famous Atlantic liners. Classed as an intermediate liner, she made scheduled sailings from Liverpool to New York, commencing with her maiden voyage on 17 June 1939, and also acted as substitute for each of the *Queens* while they were undergoing refits. Although she was placed on the Liverpool to New York service, she became the largest liner to use the Pool of London when she entered the King George V Dock on 6 August 1939. By December of 1939 she was laid up in New York but by the following March she had been taken up as a troopship by the Government and sailed to Sydney for conversion. She was returned to Cunard in September 1946 and then overhauled by her builders, making her first postwar voyage on 26 April 1947. During December 1962, after she had been committed to mainly cruise employment, the *Mauretania* was painted in the light green livery that had been introduced with Cunard's *Caronia*. After only three years in this role she became surplus to requirements and on 23 November 1965 arrived at Inverkeithing for demolition. The photograph shows the *Mauretania* in her original colour scheme departing Southampton for New York. *Kenneth Wightman*

Back cover:
RANGITATA
(10/1929) New Zealand Shipping Co
16,969grt; 552ft 5in (168.4m) loa x 78ft 9in (24.0m) beam
100 First-class, 85 Second-class and 410 Third-class
John Brown & Co, Clydebank
2 x Oil 2SA 6-cyl Doxford (by builder): 10,500bhp

Second of three sisters introduced to the Southampton to Wellington service in the late 1920s, the *Rangitata* commenced her maiden voyage on 22 November 1929. Like her sisters, *Rangitane* and *Rangitiki*, the *Rangitata* participated in the Children's Overseas Reception Board (CORB) evacuation scheme in 1940, taking 113 children to foster homes in New Zealand. Thereafter, she was requisitioned as a troopship. Prior to a complete refit in 1948-49, the *Rangitata* carried emigrants to New Zealand. She resumed her owner's passenger service from London on 23 September 1949. Twelve years later, on 3 May 1962, she arrived at London at the end of her last commercial voyage. Sold to Dutch breakers, she was re-sold to a Yugoslav concern, making the delivery voyage to the scrapyard in Split under the temporary name *Rang*. The *Rangitata* and her sisters represented a step improvement in the standard of passenger service linking the United Kingdom and New Zealand. They were also among a group of liners introduced in those years that helped to establish the internal combustion engine as the prime mover for large passenger vessels on long-haul voyages. This photograph shows the *Rangitata* berthed in the King George V Dock, London. *Kenneth Wightman*

ACKNOWLEDGEMENTS
David Clark
Mick Lindsay
Southampton Central Library – Maritime & Special Collections

BIBLIOGRAPHY & SOURCES
British Passenger Liners by Laurence Dunn (Adlard Coles)
Canadian Pacific by George Musk (World Ship Society)
The Cape Run by W H Mitchell & L A Sawyer (Terence Dalton)
Cunard Portraits by John H Isherwood (World Ship Society)
The Decline and Revival of the British Passenger Fleet by Nick Robbins (Colourpoint)
Disasters at Sea by Milton H Watson (Patrick Stephens)
Famous Liners of the Past-Belfast Built by Laurence Dunn (Adlard Coles)
Glory Days: Cunard and *Glory Days: P&O* by David Williams (Ian Allan)
Great Passenger Ships of the World – volumes 1-6 by Arnold Kludas (Patrick Stephens)
The Last Atlantic Liners by William Miller (Conway Maritime Press)
The Last Blue Water Liners by William Miller (Conway Maritime Press)
Modern Shipping Disasters, 1963-1987 by Norman Hooke (Lloyds of London Press)
Passenger Ships of the Orient Line by Neil McCart (Patrick Stephens)
20th Century Passenger Ships of the P&O by Neil McCart (Patrick Stephens)
P&O – A Fleet History by Stephen Rabson & Kevin O'Donoghue (World Ship Society)
Shaw Savill & Albion by Richard de Kerbrech (Conway Maritime Press)
Ships of the Seven Seas by Charles Graham (Ian Allan)
Warships of World War II by H T Lenton & J J College (Ian Allan)
Wartime Disasters at Sea by David Williams (Patrick Stephens)

Lloyd's Registers - various
Merchant Fleets in Profile – various volumes by Duncan Haws (Patrick Stephens)
Ocean Ships – various editions by H M Le Fleming or Bert Moody (Ian Allan)

www.clydesite.co.uk/clydebuilt
www.greatoceanliners.net
www.red-duster.co.uk
www.theshipslist.com